PENGUIN BOOKS

YOU DON'T SUCK

It's not where you start, it's how you move forward with purpose.

A programme director at work, a coach by passion, and a writer at heart, Allison Ching abides by the mantra 'Dream, Do, Deliver' and hopes to inspire this conviction in her readers and the people she meets to impact their lives and help them to achieve their goals.

Allison started her career as a news and business editor. After several years, she decided to pursue an MBA with INSEAD Business School to broaden her capabilities and opportunities. Polished in programme management, relationship management, and communications, Allison has launched and scaled various programmes for top multi-national companies. Her goal-oriented focus and execution skills ensured major programmes achieved planned objectives and outcomes within tight timelines, winning her individual and team awards.

Allison has trained with the world's top coaching organization, Co-Active Training Institute. Passionate about developing people, she is a life coach and helps her clients progress in the areas of relationships, career, and wellness. An avid motivational speaker, Allison has won several speech competitions and was the President of Singapore's biggest professional public speaking club—Toastmasters Club of Singapore—with over 160 members during her tenure.

Allison currently works and lives in Singapore. In her free time, she writes to evoke joy, poignance, laughter, inspiration, and maybe a little controversy. She is happiest when she is lost in her imagination, wandering among trees, eating spicy local delights, and when she finally masters the piano one day.

You Don't Suck
The new A to Z to make it!

Allison Ching

PENGUIN BOOKS
An imprint of Penguin Random House

PENGUIN BOOKS

USA | Canada | UK | Ireland | Australia
New Zealand | India | South Africa | China | Southeast Asia

Penguin Books is part of the Penguin Random House group of companies
whose addresses can be found at global.penguinrandomhouse.com

Published by Penguin Random House SEA Pte Ltd
9, Changi South Street 3, Level 08-01,
Singapore 486361

First published in Penguin Books by Penguin Random House SEA 2023
Copyright © Allison Ching 2023

ISBN 9789815127850

Typeset in Adobe Caslon Pro by MAP Systems, Bangalore, India

www.penguin.sg

To my parents, who are my biggest fans,
and my husband Benjamin, for his patience, love, and support.

Contents

Introduction

Congratulations!

You made it here. How you arrive at this point in your life is a result of countless actions and decisions. Where you go from this point to the next also consists of countless actions and decisions. Wherever your destination is, remember, our lives are defined by a series of actions and decisions, not just one.

I wish that I had learnt the above much earlier. I made a couple of poor choices in my late teens. For a long period in my twenties, I was so unhappy that I yearned for a do-over. I underestimated what I could do to turn things around and overestimated the impact of those choices. It led to my career being stagnant, my salary being stagnant, and my life being stagnant. I explored options half-heartedly to improve my situation, but I was going nowhere. I did not stick with what I wanted to do. I lacked focus, but the biggest reason is:

I didn't have a goal.

Part of me was scared and lost. I was scared to think about a goal because I didn't think I would ever know how to reach it. I was lost. I had no idea where to start. It's like figuring out how to own a Ferrari when you can't even afford a scooter.

Now, speaking as a person who has achieved many goals—such as getting into a prestigious business school, owning my own home by thirty—and enjoying the fruits of my labour, I dare say that having a goal is absolutely necessary, no matter how daunting those goals may seem. Bet on your future and not against it. Believe me, you have what it takes. So, start setting your goals to bring yourself from where you are now to where you dream to be.

Here comes the next part.

How do you reach your goal?

Let's face it. Only a handful of people achieved what they had set out to do. Are you one of those who did or those who didn't?

Even if you belong to the latter group, don't worry, you are not alone. Just ask around, how many people have achieved their New Year resolutions?

Let's use one of the most common resolutions—lose weight and get fit. Imagine if everyone who wants to lose weight or get fit signs up for a gym membership and goes to the gym diligently, there will be overcapacity, and everything will be over-utilized! There is a reason why gyms and other membership clubs operate smoothly—they are funded by inactive members. Gyms will not be able to operate if every member goes there daily. They count on this principle that most members are inactive or will drop out and therefore kiss goodbye to their lose weight and get fit resolutions[1].

You must be wondering, what is the point of setting a goal only to fail?

---

[1] USA Today reported in 2016 that 67 per cent of gym memberships are not used. Among those who do use their gym membership, many are not regulars.

Because you won't.

Because you can do it.

The line between success and failure hinges on a handful of factors. If you are aware of them, accept them, and apply them, then you can reach your goals. I did it, and I am about to tell you what I wish somebody had told me two decades ago.

What this book is about

This book explores the realities of what it takes to achieve your goals while inspiring you to become a fulfilled and better person through this journey. In this exploration, you will find:

- timeless truths,
- unconventional perspectives,
- popular research and studies,
- light-hearted and serious examples,
- personal and second-hand experiences,
- practical approaches and advice,
- and simple wisdom for thought.

Through the above, I hope to bring you clarity, conviction, and courage to forge ahead. You don't need to be rich, beautiful, or talented to appreciate or to apply the learnings. Nothing in this book is beyond the means of you and me. To achieve a goal, multiple factors must be considered and set up. Fortunately, these factors revolve around you—your mindset, your actions, your reactions, your choices, and your motivation—this means it is in *your hands* to pave your own path.

I have arrived at my desired state through a winding road, but you do not have to experience the frustrations and anguish I did. I compiled my knowledge and experiences and captured the learnings in this book and still consistently apply them today to reach newer goals. With the right knowledge, guidance, and motivation, you are poised to savour success quicker and easier.

How to read this book

Although I presented the chapters in this book alphabetically for easier recall of each message, they are grouped broadly under three sections. I will point out that very rarely the chapters are self-contained. It's due to the fluidity of the messages and this is a perfect example that evergreen lessons know no boundaries. However, if you prefer, you are welcome to read each chapter independently for your specific learnings. Please note that the chapters in this book will vary in length depending on the points made. The anecdotes and examples in the book are inspired and based on real stories but pseudonyms are used to protect the identities of the people mentioned.

Setting up (Chapters A–G, K, Y)

Adopt an optimal and expansive mindset and attitude to set yourself up for success. Understand the inner conditioning that is required to achieve your goals. Gain fresh and enlightened perspectives of yourselves, others, situations, and life. Any goal attainment begins with transformation, and it starts inwards. Face and conquer your inner procrastinator, saboteur, and victim who are holding you back. Get going and take charge of your life.

Sustaining (Chapters H–J, L–Q)

Consider and explore various strategies, approaches, and options to support and advance your goals. There are difficulties, but there are also possibilities. I will share what has worked for me and others. Whether or not the advice or suggestions directly apply to you, they can help generate new ideas, heighten your awareness, minimize disruption, sustain yourself efficiently, or even turn things around. The more your mind is expanded, the more frequent insights, inspirations, and epiphanies appear. These can shift your beliefs, which in turn shift your actions, and ultimately shift your results.

Reflecting (Chapters R–X, Z)

Pause and contemplate what is ahead. People can experience burnout, doubt, or even emptiness at any stage of the journey. It is important to reflect, recharge, and renew your focus. At the same time, take this opportunity to review your goals and motivations, challenge existing perspectives, and question your knowledge. There are lessons to guide you through mixed emotions and fog to release your final mental or emotional blockers before continuing the journey or moving on to a newer one.

What to take note of

While you may be applying the learnings actively, please note that positive changes take time and achieving your goals will not happen overnight. It requires consistent effort, perseverance, patience, and sometimes luck.

We all face or possess different things, be it our circumstances, personalities, or capabilities. There will be other things which you need to adopt or adapt to suit your unique situation. There are no universal results, but there are evergreen lessons in this book that can support your journey.

You choose what works best for you.

In your attempt to reach your goal, you will find no prescribed path. You have to seek your own way. Each decision and each action come with pros and cons. You have to be truthful to yourself, you have to make an effort, and you have to believe that you own your fate.

Life is full of contradictions, delayed gratifications, and unexpected twists and turns. No one, not even you, knows how your life will unfold. But come what may, I hope you will always remember the precious lessons as you progress towards your goals.

Dear readers, I wish you luck in the actions you choose, the goals you hope to achieve, and the force to take you through. We have more options than the generations who came before us; all we need is *the will*.

Lead your life, and don't let your life lead you.

Chapter A
Act Now

'You are not judged by your intentions, you're judged by your actions.'

—Mrs Goh, my high school teacher
who gave me detention for missing a class
despite my pleas that I did so to study well
for her upcoming test

The world looks at your actions, pays you for your actions, and remembers you for your actions.

Act towards your goal

The first step towards action is to get out of bed. Easier said than done? There is a reason why the snooze button was invented. You can't change your situation by staying still. While you may feel like a pair of invisible hands is holding you down, you need to muster every ounce of energy to move from a state of inertia to a state of movement. Inertia resides in your mind, and that is where you need to start targeting.

Acknowledge what you want

Acknowledgement builds energy and legitimacy. You want to awaken the dormant energy within you. You want to get serious. If you believe in quantum physics, the world is composed of countless atoms charged with energy, and they attract energy with similar composition. The thoughts in your mind are filled with such atoms. By awakening the dormant energy inside you and focusing your mind on what you want, you attract the type of energy that you require to support your goals. Start by writing down your goals and, very importantly, be specific when you do so.

Clarity convinces

Imagine if you have a limited budget of $3,000 to appoint one person to organize a team outing for 18–20 people. Your colleague Tom suggested he would like to use the money to organize food and drinks at a restaurant plus some entertainment. Another colleague Jerry told you that he would like to start the day with a scavenger hunt game, followed by an international buffet dinner at the Ritz, and end the night with Karaoke at XYZ centre, all within the budget. Who are you likely to appoint?

I hope we are unanimous on this decision. Not only does Jerry sound clearer about his plan, but he also saves you time and effort in asking follow-up questions on restaurant location and type of entertainment.

Likewise, it makes a difference when you merely wish for something versus when you clearly articulate what you want. If you can't articulate your goal clearly, how do you convince yourself and others that you really want it? Clarity is pivotal to directing your focus and energy to summon the resources and support you need to obtain your goal.

What's in a goal?

Instead of a general goal such as *I want to buy a car*, write *I will buy a red Audi e-tron S Sportback as a birthday gift to myself by June 26, 2024*. Similarly, if you are looking for a job in healthcare, be specific about the role, the company, the location, and so on.

SMART goals

This is a tried and tested framework created by George T. Doran, Arthur Miller and James Cunningham in 1981 to help people to clarify, define, and manage their goals.

S	M	A	R	T
Specific	Measurable	Achievable	Relevant	Time-bound

This is a tool that many project managers use, including myself. SMART stands for Specific, Measurable, Achievable, Relevant, and Time-bound.

When writing your goals, be sure to consider:

- How specific are my goals for me to take appropriate actions?
- Am I able to measure my progress and results objectively?
- Can I achieve my goals? They should not be impossible to achieve.
- How relevant and aligned are my current goals to my broader goals and purpose?
- What is the time I need to achieve my goals?

Examples of SMART goals are:

- I will be a software engineer with Google and work at their corporate campus in Mountain View by 2026.
- I will weigh 55 kg, decrease my BMI to 20, and be a size 8 by next July.
- I will graduate from culinary school in 2024 and open my first Spanish seafront restaurant at the beach in Seminyak, Bali, by 2027.
- I will spend the first weekend of every month with my parents at their countryside home near Elm Lake.

Visualize: What you see is what you get

If you can visualize it, you have already done it. At least that is what your brain thinks.

If you are finding it hard to be specific about your goal in the above segment, visualization can help you. Visualization provides the initial clarity to get you started. Let's first understand how it works.

Visualization activates the power of the subconscious mind, one of the most powerful inner forces. It drives behaviour and thoughts in various ways to reconcile your current reality with your visualization. When you visualize an action, you stimulate the same part of the brain as if you are actually performing the action. The brain gets activated and trained in the same manner.

A lemon-tasting test

Close your eyes and imagine the following. You are holding a lemon close to your mouth, gently squeezing the lemon, and sucking the juice. It tastes sour and bitter. Keep this image until your saliva glands react to the lemon's taste. When you open your eyes, do you notice your saliva building up? Even without tasting a real lemon, your body reacts like you are!

Research has shown that the brain does not differentiate between what is real and what is imagined or visualized. Hence, when you visualize something vividly, your brain registers that visualization as a real memory.

Swing it

Visualization is also a commonly used technique in sports. Golf is one such sport.

Many golfers—be it my husband, my coach, or PGA champions—use visualization to aid their game. One of the greatest golfers of all time, the Golden Bear, Jack Nicklaus said, 'I never hit a shot, not even in practice, without having a very sharp in-focus picture of it in my head.'

If you've done it before, you tend to get better the second, third, or fourth time. Visualization allows you to re-do, re-play, and re-live that experience, even if it's mentally! Continuing with the example of golf, to carry out the visualization effectively, you must visualize not just the outcome, but the whole scenario, such as your physical movements, the environment, and the destination. This would mean imagining your stance, the iron (type of golf club) you are holding, your physical environment, your eyes on the tee, and—as you swing—the ball landing at the exact point where you want it to be!

How to do visualization

1. To start, it can be as simple as closing your eyes and visualizing that you have attained your goals. Where are you? What are you doing?
2. If that image is slightly fuzzy, add some senses to the image.
   - What do you see when you have attained your goal? If you are visualizing owning a car, imagine the colour, the model, the interior, the wheels, and so on.
   - Continuing with the car example, what do you hear when you drive? How is the sound of the horn?
   - How are the seats? What does the leather smell like?
   - What is the sensation of driving on a highway? Do you like the wind brushing your face with the windows open?
3. Incorporate emotions into your visualization. They fuel your visualization and make it more real. If your goal

> is to buy a loft apartment in the city, and you are visualizing yourself inside the apartment, how do you feel? Are you exhilarated? Are you proud to be a homeowner?
> 4. Do this every morning when you wake up and every evening before you sleep to reinforce your visualization.

The concept will begin to feel more real and achievable when you replay the scenarios and interact with the various senses. You pre-position yourself for actual situations when they arise because you have already practised and trained for them in your mind. Gradually, the wheels are turning in one part of your brain to affect the other parts to take intended actions and select options that count towards making your visualizations a reality.

Manifesting my goals

I went one step further to strengthen my visualization. I had two major goals in the last decade. Call it luck, call it motivation, call it visualization, I achieved both of them.

My first goal was to get into a prestigious business school. I did the steps above, and I visited the school! I went to the auditoriums, the canteen, the hallways, everywhere. I sat in the auditorium, touched the desk, pretended that there was a professor in front of me, and even imagined myself dozing off during lectures! Seeing, hearing, and feeling the physical surroundings helped tremendously in my visualization. The rest is history.

My second goal was to own an apartment in a central and classy location. After looking at several apartments, I found a condominium in a district that I really fancied. The issues were, no surprises, the prices of the apartments and non-negotiable homeowners! The first two apartments I viewed in that condominium and made offers for did not go through as the owners would not budge on prices. I love the facilities and the neighbourhood, and I just could not bear the thought of not being able to afford staying there. I went back to the neighbourhood several times, walked from the metro station to the condominium, and visualized those 400 metres as my daily route. Call it the third time lucky, I found a fantastic apartment, better than the first two, on the top floor. After a series of tough negotiations, the owner relented and agreed to sell me the apartment for close to $150,000 below his asking price!

If you lack something concrete to reinforce your visualization, there are other ways to enhance it and get as close to your desired reality as possible. Look at magazines, watch television shows, go online to search for related images, watch videos on YouTube, or find a substitute close to it, be it a location, an object, or an image that best represents it. Visualize with your senses and emotions. All you need is creativity and determination.

Be reminded every day and every chance you get

After you have successfully visualized your goal(s) in detail, write it down on a piece of paper and pin it to your fridge, record it on your audio journal and play it regularly, put the image related to the goal as your screensaver, note it in your online calendar and set notifications, or announce your goal to your friends and family so that they can keep you accountable. Be surrounded by images and echoes of your goals to stay committed. Subconsciously, your mind will channel your attention and help you focus your energy on things needed to get you towards your goal.

Set yourself up for action

If there is something new you wish to bring into your life, you have to create space for it—be it physically, emotionally, or mentally. Begin by decluttering. Mess competes for your attention and limits your ability to focus, let alone act. Get organized and carve out a space. Re-arrange as you wish and remove all temptations and unwanted reminders. They come in all forms. It can be an ashtray if you aim to quit smoking, the XXXL jeans in a corner of your cupboard, or gifts from a past relationship. Remove remnants that can tie you to the past or down in the present. You want to move ahead! Designate a new object or a spot that signals action towards your goal. Preparing your space serves as a cue to prime the brain, heart, and every inch of the fibre in your body to get ready to act.

Another way to declutter and take your mind off things is to transfer the floating thoughts in your mind onto paper. Write down a list of things you need to do. Penning down your thoughts helps free you of the responsibility to remember them. In addition, you are making the intangible tangible. When you see what you have to do, it gives you the impetus to act.

Acting and planning moves you closer to reality

When you have the list of items, it is time to create a plan. Planning helps to gel the various items and give more clarity to the road ahead. It also pushes you to think about the 'how' so you can determine resources, actions, and timelines, as well as the relevant metrics and feedback methods to track your progress. I will not go into comprehensive project management 101. However, I have guidelines, accumulated over a decade of project management experience, to help you think through what you need to start giving your goal plan more structure. Having a plan eliminates ambiguity and randomness that hinder you from moving forward.

How to plan for your goal(s)

1. **Arrange, prioritize, and assess**
    This point applies if you have more than one goal. Assess what your short versus long-term goals are. Does one goal have to be achieved before you can go on to the next one, or can you go about them simultaneously? I suggest focusing on one goal at a time, especially if it requires significant effort or if you are not sure to be able to adjust right away to a new routine brought about by the goal(s).

2. **Set a realistic time frame**
    You wish to be stretched, but you also wish to be realistic. Do you intend to achieve a particular goal in six months, one, two, five, or ten years? Pay attention to goals with a shelf life due to age, health, and especially if they are determined by external parties such as entry to competitions. In addition, set milestones at suitable intervals to ensure you progress at the right pace. Without milestones, it's difficult to ascertain if you are on schedule or behind schedule in the first year if the time frame to achieve your goal is in a decade.

3. **Write down the list of things**
    There are two specific components to this—an item list and a to-do list—basically what you need and what you have to do. For example, if your goal is to be able to play the piano, you will require these items. I have kept the list simple for illustrative purposes and it is not exhaustive:
    *   A piano
    *   Money to buy the piano and pay for the lessons
    *   Space to put the piano
    *   Time for the lessons and practicing the piano

What you have to do:

- Seek advice and recommendations from your friends who play the piano and decide how you wish to go about it.
- Find a teacher and school.
- Allocate time in your schedule for regular lessons and practice.
- Cultivate and deepen interest through attending concerts and listening to piano music.

The lists can be very long, depending on your goals. Some goals may necessitate learning a new skill or obtaining some form of qualification. Do not be put off by it. Be clear about what you need and have faith that you will muster all the resources and strength to support you.

4. **Put them all together**

Project management! Getting the blocks of things aligned with the timelines at different stages is crucial to building a strong base for your take-off.

- Set an overall timeline with milestones.
- Designate a start and end date for each task. Schedule what you need to do this week, month, or quarter.
- Consider dependencies. Some tasks can be done simultaneously whereas others require one or more other tasks to be completed or started before you can begin work on them.
- Identify possible obstacles and risks that can hinder your progress. Make sure you plan some buffer or think about mitigation measures to reduce any impact.

5.   Track and review your progress
     It is extremely important to monitor your progress at
     each phase. You want to know what is completed and
     what still needs to be accomplished. Take this chance
     to appraise the overall journey, including timeline,
     dependencies, issues, and others. What are your
     learnings? Are there any areas you wish to refine?
6.   **Refine your goals**
     Due to a myriad of reasons, almost everyone will go
     through this step even with considerations and buffers
     for obstacles and risks incorporated in the original plan.
     You can't expect the plan to remain static from start
     to end. Hence, what is more important is your ability
     to be agile and adaptable to change while keeping
     your focus. Through constant review and reflection
     on your progress, you are able to evolve your plan as
     circumstances shift.

A concrete plan + determined actions = Recipe for success.

A little action is better than no action

Be aware that even with all things laid out, inertia happens
to the best of us. At any point, when you encounter inertia,
I advise you to take the path of least resistance. As much as
jumping into the deep end of the pool is not the ideal way to
learn to swim, thinking about weighty tasks is probably not the
best way to draw you into action. Hence, look for the easiest or
tiniest task. Once you have completed the task, you will have
warmed up to the work. For example, if you find it difficult to

shrug off your lethargy to exercise, tell yourself to walk for just five minutes. You will be more inclined to continue once you start moving.

'Success is 10% inspiration and 90% perspiration.'
—Thomas Edison, one of the most prolific
inventors of all time

What is in the 90 per cent perspiration?

Action.

Energy generates momentum, momentum generates actions, and actions generate more energy. Harness the energy within you to act. Remember, nothing happens until you act. Get rid of your inner snooze button. The key to your goal is to act; the best time to start is *now*.

Act now.

Key takeaways

- Everything begins from inside your mind. Get into the state of mind of action.
- Clarity in articulating your goals is pivotal to directing your focus and energy. Use SMART goals as a guide.
- Use visualization to activate the power of the subconscious mind to imagine you are living your desired reality.
- A concrete plan is key to organizing your activities. It also helps in tracking your progress.
- Action generates energy which generates more action. Little action is better than no action. Keep moving.

Chapter B
Be Bold and Believe

'If you do not believe you can do it, then you have no chance at all.'

—Arsène Wenger, longest-serving manager
of the Arsenal football team

How often do you dream of getting from A–Z only to have an inner voice telling you, *Wow that is really bold, I'm not sure if it's possible. I think you should just aim to get to B or C*?

If you want to go for Z, you must believe that you have what it takes to get there. *Being bold with your goals is not the same as being unrealistic.* People sometimes confuse the two.

If you want to quit your stable software engineering job and become a successful restaurateur, that's bold, and not unrealistic.

If you are terrified of public speaking but aspire to become a litigator, that's bold, not unrealistic.

If you are overweight but you want to get fit and run a marathon, that's bold, not unrealistic.

Being unrealistic is setting big audacious goals without a purpose and a plan.

What you want and why you want it

I spoke about goal clarity in the previous chapter. After you know what you want, you must know why you want it. What is it about the goal that is fulfilling for you? Your purpose is your *why* and it's also the compass that will guide you to your goal. When you pursue something aligned with your purpose, you will do so with more tenacity and passion. You feel right, you feel joy, and you feel that everything is in balance. There is no inner conflict that will pull you away from your quest.

Having clarity in your purpose will serve you in planning the resources, actions, and timeline, as well as dealing with other challenges along the way. The devil is in the details, and managing this devil is draining. With purpose, you are determined. You will reset your life and organize your activities around the purpose to try and attain your goal. You are doing what you love, and what you do means so much to you that you are willing to go all the way for it, even when you are exhausted and even when the going gets extremely tough.

Who else but you? You have to believe

If what you want really resonates with you and makes your body tingle with excitement, then you must believe in yourself and that it's possible. What people think about your ideas or dreams is none of your business. For instance, if business magnate Fred Smith, then a Yale University undergraduate, had been discouraged by a 'C' on his paper on using planes to transport items, he would never have founded FedEx, a global transportation company, and become the CEO. Don't let anyone talk you out of believing. If you limit your goals to only what you think is possible or what others say is possible, then you get what you deserve.

Have the self-fulfilling prophecy work for you in a positive way. A self-fulfilling prophecy is the outcome of a situation shaped by our thinking. So, think positively! Your beliefs influence your actions and behaviour, which in turn influence the outcome in the way you expect them to be.

The haunted forest

One day, Lassie, a dog well-loved by the villagers, went missing. Frantic, the villagers decided to split and look for Lassie.

Tom, one of the villagers, found a trail and decided to follow it. He was so focused on following the trail that he didn't realize he was entering a forest.

A few villagers, who saw Tom approaching the forest, began to shout hysterically.

'Stop, Tom, stop! No one is supposed to go into the forest!'

'The forest is haunted! Come back!'

'You'll get into trouble and die! Don't be silly!'

As the villagers watched Tom disappear into the forest, they stopped in their tracks, too shocked to do anything.

Minutes later, Tom emerged from the forest, bringing Lassie along. The villagers were both relieved to see both him and Lassie unharmed and quickly surround him.

'Thank goodness you are safe! Didn't you hear us shouting?'

'What did you say?' responded Tom. 'I forgot to turn on my hearing aid.'

Sometimes, you just have to turn a deaf ear to tune out negative comments.

You always have it in you

You always have a leader inside of you. You need to harness it. Tap into your inner leader, the figure in command who is fearless, composed, wise, and who directs your journey in alignment with your purpose. Your inner leader is part of who you are and who you are becoming and is committed to helping you to become more resilient and effective. At any given moment, you can always draw on the courageous and resourceful traits of your inner leader to manage the situation.

From the point of view of your inner leader, reflect on your strengths, personality, qualities, values, and passion. What are you most proud of? What can you accept about yourself?

Embrace what makes you unique. Within our inner leader is a self that plays different roles, such as a warrior, a friend, a cheerleader, and many more. Channel that role which serves you best in dealing with any situation. The spirit of your inner leader is committed to helping you succeed.

Fear is scary, and that's normal

'Too many of us are not living our dreams because we are living our fears.'
                    —Les Brown, dynamic motivational speaker

A big reason why many people don't dare to go all out for their goals is because of fear. They fear obstacles, they fear working hard, they fear failure, they fear change, they fear the unknown, and the list is never-ending.

To set goals means having to enter unchartered territory. The unknown can be frightening. Things just got real. You need to make new plans, you have more to consider, you are under more scrutiny, you face more pressure, and you have to step up your game.

One way to handle fear is to understand it. Understand that fear is normal and can be useful. Fear helps to protect us through hardwiring survival instincts within our system to alert impending danger. Apart from nature, we learn to fear since childhood through various influences from our environment or culture, such as the conditioning from your overprotective parents or the limiting beliefs that they have inherited and passed on to you that thwarts your courage to venture into new areas.

Shina's fear

I had a neighbour whom I was quite close to growing up back in my old flat. Let us call her Shina.

Shina's family was financially challenged. Every time she asked them for pocket money or additional money to buy essentials for school, she would get yelled at or, at best, nagged by her parents. Shina grew up never daring to ask for anything, especially money. I had to convince her to approach her boss for pay raise and even her ex-boss for late salary payments. Shina associated asking for money or anything with pain and avoided that like the plague due to her childhood influences.

In 2007, I invited her to the Millionaire Mind Intensive seminar after reading the book *Secrets of the Millionaire Mind* by T. Harv Eker. The book talks about our internal financial blueprint that's ingrained into the subconscious and that what we associate money with will determine our financial destiny. I was inspired by it, and I hoped that the seminar would help her.

It did!

Change took some time, but Shina realized what caused her to hold back and eventually confronted her fears. She fervently pursued and got a role as a journalist that compensated well and led her to settle in Melbourne, Australia.

Fear is also developed through negative experiences or close observations. Limitless things happened to us during the process of growing up. We realized that life wouldn't always bring us smoothly from one point to another. It's true that we don't always get what we want even when we try hard. We hit bumps, we tumble, and those falls hurt. After a few falls, we start to become guarded. We want to outsmart getting hurt, so we constantly build a fence between where we are and where we think we may fall. Our minds communicate fear because they remember the undesirable incidents more vividly and wish to protect us by constantly signalling the dangers.

From this, you can see that fear exists for many reasons. If you understand fear, you will see that it's simply a protective mental barrier programmed naturally into us and also a by-product of our life experiences.

Fear is not something to be avoided. It is something to be accepted.

CartoonStock.com

Personify your fear and talk to it

Accepting that fear is normal does not mean you let fear run you. Think of fear as a saboteur that holds you back from realizing your potential. It manifests through language such as *I can't, I don't, and I shouldn't*. It's the voice of disapproval and negativity that attempts to maintain the status quo and defeat your will to move forward. You need to face it, control it, and overcome it. Start by recognizing its presence and voice.

You want to quit your engineering job and start a business? *What if you fail and end up in debt? Your family is going to suffer for your decision!*

You are afraid of public speaking but wish to be a litigator? *Imagine getting cold feet in front of the judge. You're going to embarrass yourself!*

You are overweight but wish to get fit and run a marathon? *You're going to wake up two hours earlier just to go to the gym? You could get hurt by brisk walking!*

The more you train yourself to be aware of your inner saboteur, the more you recognize its sneaky attempts to ruin your goals and dreams. Take note of the circumstances when your saboteur tends to appear and see if you can find patterns.

To make your saboteur more conspicuous, give it a form. What does it look like? What is its tone? What feelings does it evoke in you? Find or create an artefact that represents them, such as a figurine. Whenever your saboteur shows up, talk to it. Find out what it wants from you.

Acknowledge its presence and recognize that it's just doing its job to protect you. Finally, thank your saboteur for sharing its thoughts and reminding you of the danger and then put it away.

Don't forget to call upon your inner leader. They are powerful, especially when dealing with a saboteur, because they help to fight it with your resolute purpose, supported by allies of courage, acceptance, and compassion. Access your strengths and brilliance and break your limits to go after what you truly want.

Being bold pays off

No matter how far your goal seems, how humble your start is, or how many tiny steps you need to take, don't be afraid to set your sights high and go for it.

> 'A goal should scare you a little and excite you a lot.'
> —Joe Vitale, spiritual teacher best known
> for his appearance in the movie
> *The Secret* and as the author of
> *The Attractor Factor*

You stretch your limits and explore your potential

By attempting new challenges and adapting to new experiences, you are simultaneously building a unique repertoire of knowledge and skill sets. You gain new information, fresh perspectives, and stronger self-awareness. Essayist and philosopher Ralph Waldo Emerson said, 'The mind, once stretched by a new idea, never returns to its original dimensions.' Don't short-change yourself and disconnect from what you truly want. Shoot for the stars and see where you land.

You can see how far you have come, even if you fall short

You may have yet to reach your intended goal, but you gave it all and went the farthest you could. You landed somewhere, and this is just the beginning. It's not uncommon to go through a lengthy process or trial and err multiple times before you attain your goal. It's not always about succeeding at all costs, it's about learning and getting back on your feet every time on the way to your destination.

Jasmine's dancing dream

Speaking of feet, my childhood friend Jasmine has always dreamt of being a professional ballerina. However, she was overweight and was told by the teacher that she should become much leaner before enrolling in classes. The news crushed her, but she was so determined to become a ballerina that she did all kinds of sports to slim down. She eventually lost about 25 kg by her teens. But guess what? Unfortunately, she broke her left ankle and both her legs during a freak sports accident and was advised by her doctor not to pursue ballet or professional dancing as a career. Despite her desire, she never went on to fulfil her dream of becoming a ballerina.

Given her slight handicap, I was surprised that she later joined a social dance club and invited me for an evening. When I arrived, she was already on the dance floor. I stared at her uncoordinated moves and thought, 'Thank God she never became a ballerina!' Still, I was amazed by her spirit given her setback. I approached her and asked, 'Are you okay to dance now? I thought you had a problem with your legs?'

She replied with a smile, 'I love to dance. Just because I can't dance well doesn't mean I shouldn't dance.'

Did Jasmine fall short of her ballerina dream? Yes.

Is Jasmine content? You betcha. She was in greater spirits than I thought.

Jasmine's story continues in a later chapter.

Sometimes you can only recognize what you truly want when you get there

Let's assume that you have succeeded in opening several restaurants. However, after some time, you realize that running a business does not fulfil you and takes your focus and time away from doing what you enjoy, which is creating innovative recipes that delight your customers. Hence, you decide to sell most of your restaurants and devote time to being a head chef in just one. Being bold is not necessarily about chasing bigger and more stuff, it's also about keeping what matters most and letting go of the rest.

You will feel genuinely rewarded

The wave of euphoria and the sense of pride that comes with achieving the goals that mean so much to you are unparalleled. Don't compromise that feeling and opt to pursue something lesser because you fear you can't obtain the big one. You shouldn't be afraid to dream, so dream big.

'You become what you believe.'
—Oprah Winfrey, host of *The Oprah Winfrey Show*

Key takeaways

- Don't be afraid to dream and set bold goals. Being bold with your goals is not the same as being unrealistic.
- Knowing your purpose—the 'why'—will get you through the tough times.
- Draw on your inner leader for strength and tenacity to help you succeed.
- Fear is normal and merely a protective mental barrier programmed naturally into us. Channel your inner leader to manage and control your fear.
- Only by being bold and going after your goals will you stretch your limits, discover yourself, and experience the full range of emotions.

Chapter C

Complain if You Must, but Get Over It Soon

'Spending today complaining about yesterday won't make tomorrow any better.'

—Unknown

You may want to let it all out . . .

To move from one point to another en route to your goal requires change. You need to change your habits, routine, environment, or even friends. Change can cause inconvenience, stress, and pain. Although it's understandable to feel anxious and frustrated initially, you should not hold on to these pent-up negative feelings as they are insidious and detrimental to your emotional, mental, and physical health.

You need to blow off steam. If complaining is your sure and immediate channel to release your stress, then do it. After all, it can be a useful way to process emotions. You're like a shaken can of carbonated drink with all the pressure that needs to pop. Letting it out relieves the inner tension. Complaining can be healing, even for a moment. Sometimes you just need to dispel the negative energy before facing the situation. After venting, you feel calmer.

. . . but don't get addicted

Like all things, there is a line to be drawn. If you are complaining incessantly without the intention of moving on from your frustrations, you are simply reliving your aggravation. As long as you keep focusing and lamenting on what makes you unhappy, you create and attract the same type of energy that ties you to your present unhappy state, allowing your complaints to overpower your ambitions. Hence, it's vital to self-manage before this behaviour becomes habitual.

For example, do you exhibit one or more of the following signs?

- You grumble but you don't attempt to find any solution.
- You dwell on past situations.
- You become frequently and easily irritated.
- You have a negative outlook on where things are going.
- You alienate your loved ones.

If your answer is yes to one or more of the above, it's time to consider a few measures.

(i) Set a time limit to adjust

Depending on your goal, give yourself a reasonable time to adjust. Change takes time to get used to, but you need to ensure that this behaviour is temporary and does not become chronic. In the meantime, you can find a healthier way to release tension through music, sports, cooking, or any activities that relieve the pressure.

A method you can also employ to release tension is one we have discussed previously in Chapter A on visualization. To reiterate, under these practices you focus on the ideal situation you want to create and fill your mind with thoughts and sensations of the new situation. It helps shift you from a mood of frustration to satisfaction by lessening your focus on your current discomfort and envisioning a fulfilling future. Do this every time you feel your frustration piling up and spend one to two minutes visualizing and immersing yourself in the new ideal state. Gradually, you will feel your frustration dissipating and find yourself in a more neutral mood.

If you are still upset and complaining after the adjustment period, consider revisiting your goal. Perhaps this goal is incongruent with your values, perhaps it's not really what you want but what others expect of you. Additionally, our motivations are heavily influenced by our close ones, society, and the media. It's worth examining the wider associations and digging into the source to find a fix. This may require you to change your goal, but your long-term fulfilment triumphs over short-term discomfort in the grand scheme of things.

(ii) Review your plan

If your goal is not the issue, maybe your plan is. There is a possibility that your approach is wrong, your actions are harsh, your timeline is rigid, or there might be some other reasons. Consulting people, especially if they have been in your shoes, can help put things in perspective. Try revising some aspects of your plan to see if it alleviates your agony, especially if there are conflicting priorities. Reshuffle activities to fit your goal as part of your routine. In many cases, being uncomfortable is unavoidable. You learn to wrestle with it and take charge to proactively manage your situation to be in better control, so life gets easier. The key is not to be passive and simply let things happen to you.

(iii) Remember the big picture

Focus on your purpose and the reason you wanted to pursue this goal. One way to sweeten the progress is to find something enjoyable or useful to work on daily that will inch you closer to your goal. You feel happier and proud when you execute something. It reignites momentum. Sometimes all we need is to accomplish the work in front of us to make us remember why we're doing it in the first place.

In my case, I wanted to finish writing this book a year ago. However, I also experienced personal issues during the same period and had to devote much of my time to sorting them out. For a few months, I struggled to juggle my tasks, and I became miserable and frustrated until I temporarily lost the will to continue with my book. One day, I had to advise a friend on writing speeches, and that is when I realized how much I missed writing. Amid the gloom, my passion resurfaced!

Instead of wondering if I would ever finish writing my book, I simply focused on one paragraph, one chapter at a time. Well, here I am.

> Adjust with patience, review your plan, and recall your purpose.

Get rid of the victim mentality

A victim mentality is a state of mind in which people feel that they have no control over the situation that the odds are stacked against them, or that others are against them. Because they don't think that anything is their fault or are so focused on things beyond their control—instead of the many other aspects of life within their control—they become unable or are reluctant to take responsibility for what happens in their lives.

Your goal is to lose weight. You enjoy eating fried and sugary foods and complain when you gain weight instead of choosing healthier alternatives and exercising.

Your goal is to obtain a diploma in web application development. You prefer to watch TV, procrastinate on major tasks, and complain when nothing has progressed instead of getting down to action.

Your goal is to be promoted to senior manager. You want to be seen as a good employee, so you accept more and more work and complain to your friends about having no time and neglecting your family, instead of discussing work planning and allocation with your manager.

Your goal is to have a loving relationship. You are unhappy about some things in your relationship, but you don't wish to have a fight and risk breaking up, so you complain to your friends about your partner, instead of initiating a truthful conversation.

If you want to achieve something, you have to stop feeling helpless, stop complaining, and stop your excuses. We complain because we think we get something out of doing so instead of taking the harder option.

You are responsible for what's next

More often than not, it would have been you who led yourself to this present situation. Even if you are a victim of circumstances, your response to the event makes a difference. You will not get far if you continually look for faults outside of yourself to blame. Reflect on your situation and yourself. Either accept the status quo or take full responsibility for managing the consequences that come with certain choices.

There is always a silver lining. Even when things seem bleak, search for the bright side. How can you grow through this? What can you appreciate about this situation?

- You had a rough time during your cancer treatment, but through this period you realized who your true friends are and how much family matters.
- You lost your job, but you managed to take this break and attempt all the activities you didn't have time for while working.

- You dropped your bag into a canyon during a four-day hiking trip, but you learnt to survive on the barest minimum in nature. Maybe some unforgettable stories to share later!

You can't control your situation, but you can always control your response to it. Your response will determine the next outcome.

Sometimes, it pays to have the Ah Q Spirit

The term Ah Q Spirit came from Chinese writer and poet Lu Xun, a leading figure of modern Chinese literature. In his novel, *The True Story of Ah Q*, the protagonist Ah Q is known for his *spiritual victories* since he is a constant loser and has to delude himself to believe that he is successful or superior. The term is commonly used among Mandarin speakers to describe a mentality in people who see the positive side in everything, including atrocious and ridiculous situations.

One of my favourite quotes that exemplifies the Ah Q spirit is:

'I have not failed. I've just found 10,000 ways that won't work', by famous American inventor Thomas A. Edison. This quote changed my attitude and perspective. In fact, it has served me extremely well in life, work, and relationships.

'Sometimes you need to kiss many frogs before you find your prince. I have not failed. I've just found what I don't want in a man.'

'I have not failed in my job search. I've just spoken to ten companies, and I'm expecting more interviews.'

'I have not failed in learning to cook. I've just produced twenty variations to that dish.'

You only lose if you stop trying.

Today, I'm in a loving marriage, have a rewarding job, and I am a reasonably decent cook.

There are times in life when we have to accept what we don't like because we can't stop or change it. To feel better, one way to assuage our anger and misery is to adopt 'spiritual victories'. As long as you don't run away from reality permanently, it does not hurt to adopt the Ah Q spirit from time to time to console ourselves.

Be responsible for your emotions. Choose a perspective that enables you to become resilient, productive, and happy.

Put yourself in the driver's seat

I wish I could tell you that life is paved with many yellow brick roads. But we all know better that the path to your goal is lined with mixed emotions and obstacles. While complaints can be cathartic, they will never make anything better in the long term. If you are unhappy with your situation, change it. If you are unable to change the situation, manage your responses to it. Replace complaints with actions that move you in the right direction.

Maybe, you'll catch sight of your yellow brick road.

Key takeaways

- Change that comes with going after new goals is hard. Complaining may be useful for processing emotions in the short term, but don't be addicted to it.
- Self-manage by allowing yourself time to adjust, reviewing your plan, and remembering your purpose and the big picture.

- Get rid of the victim mentality and take responsibility for what happens. Be in charge of your life.
- There is a silver lining in every situation if you look for it. Choose a perspective that makes you resilient, productive, and happy.

Chapter D

Discipline, Discipline, Discipline

'Discipline is just choosing between what you want now, and what you want most.'

—Abraham Lincoln,
16th President of the United States

You just can't overlook discipline. It's one of the most powerful elements to achieve one's goals. Yet, there is no pleasant metaphor to describe discipline. It's a mental whip that strikes you so you . . .

- Start right now.
- Stay on course.
- Stop your bad habits.

Let's use a common example—losing weight—to illustrate what discipline encompasses and how to incorporate it.

Start right now

Any form of activity is good as long as it gets you in motion. In Chapter A, I mentioned taking the path of least resistance to avoid inertia. The trick is to start small and simple to warm yourself up before moving on to something bigger. A daily twenty-minute walk beats a weekly two-hour gym.

Stay on course

It takes time to form a new habit and get into a new rhythm. If you cannot exercise daily, you need to make sure you do so often enough to make it a cadence, so it will gradually be a part of your life. If you start to feel bored or uninspired, you can change your activities, find a workout buddy, or join fitness classes. There are even apps that reward you with vouchers, awards, and other goodies for hitting your fitness goals and staying on track. You have countless incentives to stay in motion.

Stop your bad habits

Diet plays a central role in losing weight. If you enjoy snacking or consuming fast food, soft drinks, or desserts, it will be detrimental to your goal. Likewise, if you are a procrastinator who postpones exercising, you will never reach your goals on time. Find ways to break your bad habits so they don't hamper your progress.

Start. Stay. Stop.

Doesn't sound so difficult, does it? So why aren't we all doing better? Let's dissect discipline to understand the mechanics behind why many people find it hard to instil discipline.

'Resistance training is just as important as cardio. Train yourself to resist chocolate, pastries, fried foods, beer, pizza....'

It's invisible

Because it's invisible, it's easy to ignore. It's difficult to quantify or measure discipline. Hence, you need to give discipline, or rather, the lack of discipline, a visible form. Continuing with the example of losing weight, one way to do so is to record what you consume. You can't change what you don't measure. You tend to underestimate your consumption if you don't input your calorie intake and witness the impact on your diet. After all, how much harm could a cute cupcake cause?

Another way is to express discipline in a quantifiable format. In Chapter A, I discussed SMART goals. You can apply the concept here by expressing discipline in an objective and measurable way. For example, discipline in controlling your weight is to exercise at least thirty minutes each time for four times a week, discipline in finding a job is to submit twelve applications every month, discipline in doubling sales revenue is to meet with twenty prospective customers every week.

When you make the invisible *visible*, you can track your progress, assess if you exceed or fall short, and be able to revise your plan because you have a baseline to work with.

It requires commitment and consistency over a period

Sustained efforts achieve wonders. You can't do as you please. You need to practise self-control and daily diligence and establish healthy habits that help you adhere to the standard and frequency required to move you towards your goals. Most of all, be prepared to do so for a sustained period of time. When I started writing this book, I didn't do it in one go! I started going through the previous stuff I've written, piecing them into paragraphs, piecing the paragraphs into chapters, writing and re-writing the chapters, writing the first version, getting reviews for it, and then rewriting it again . . . it doesn't stop there. Whenever I was not travelling, I blocked out at least one full day every weekend and some evenings after work to build up the content. The process from when I started to write to submitting my full manuscript took close to twenty months!

Discipline is mind over matter. Adjust your mindset. Believe that you can do it, you must do it, and you will do it.

Jasmine's dancing dream part 2

Remember my friend Jasmine, whom I mentioned in Chapter B, who broke her ankle and both legs and never became a ballerina? She was devastated when the doctor told her not to pursue ballet professionally. Jasmine was in a cast and crutches for almost four months. In her worst state, she had to beg the doctors to administer the maximum dosage of morphine to numb her excruciating pain.

Even after Jasmine managed to recover and walk normally, she could not match the agility of a recreational dancer, let alone go after her dream. However, Jasmine never gave up pursuing what she loved, even though she could not have it the way she originally wanted it. Her physical therapy may have ended but Jasmine would spend an hour or more working on flexibility, strengthening, and balance exercises to improve her fitness and agility every morning.

A year after I met Jasmine at the social dance club and nearly three years since her dreadful injuries, I learned that she has been participating in dance competitions. And even more amazing, she enrolled in adult ballet classes!

Jasmine is still enjoying her ballet classes and participating in dance competitions at the time of this writing. Sustained efforts do achieve wonders.

It's free

We certainly are more motivated when we pay for something. If you pay $100 an hour without refund for an acting class, you will try your best to show up. But because discipline is free, you don't feel you are wasting your money when you don't use it. Remember, if there's something more precious than money, it's *time and opportunity*. If you fail to fulfil your goals because of external factors, then tough luck. If you fail to fulfil them because you lack discipline, you have wasted your time and a potential opportunity for what could have been.

Discipline may be free, but a lack of it will cost you.

If the best things in life are free, then discipline is . . . priceless.

'Discipline, not desire, determines destiny.'
—Steve Harvey,
television host, actor, and comedian

Key takeaways

- Discipline is never pleasant, but extremely essential to achieve your goals.
- Incorporating discipline involves starting small and simple, staying consistent, and stopping bad habits.
- Expressing discipline in a quantifiable and visible format can help you track your progress.
- It takes time before you see results. Remember that sustained efforts can achieve wonders.
- You don't need to pay for discipline but lacking it will cost you and your goals.

Chapter E
Easy Does It ... NOT

'Of course it's hard. It's supposed to be hard. If it were easy, everyone would do it. Hard is what makes it great.'
—Jimmy Dugan, played by actor Tom Hanks, in the movie *In a League of Their Own*

Effort, serious effort, is needed in transformation

Before a caterpillar becomes a butterfly, it goes through metamorphosis. This process is a struggle. The butterfly must force its way out through a tiny opening in its cocoon. By doing so, it pushes the fluid out of its body and into its wings and strengthens them, enabling it to fly. If anyone tries to help by snipping the cocoon to enlarge the opening, the butterfly will emerge quicker but with a swollen body and shrivelled wings. It will never be able to fly.

Case in point.

Have you heard the phrase, 'The easy way out usually leads back in'? It's the fourth law of systems thinking mentioned in the book *The Fifth Discipline* by management guru Peter Senge. Systems thinking is an approach to looking at things and events holistically and how the various parts interrelate instead of viewing it as a single component. The idea is that things function as part of a larger context and system. Hence, by observing how they move and link, we can identify patterns and uncover the behaviour and structures. In the context of goals, they are our own mental models, habits, and values that drive these patterns and events, allowing us to devise suitable and sustainable solutions to chronic problems.

The fourth law depicts utilizing familiar solutions repeatedly while not fixing or worsening fundamental problems. Applying the law to the context of goal pursuits, we may find comfort in relying on accustomed or simpler approaches, but does it get us to where we want?

If you want your entire journey towards your goal to be effortless, it could imply:

- You've set too low a goal.
- You are unlikely to succeed.
- Your success is unlikely to be sustainable.

Choose to do it right, not to do it easy.

Successful people make it look easy

Don't be deceived by success stories out there. While these stories are a great source of learning, they also tend to sound sexier once the people have made it. The challenges and failures of entrepreneurs, celebrities, and other famous personalities in autobiographies are carefully packaged. And who's to say they don't deserve it? For example, out of a hundred aspiring entrepreneurs, you wouldn't have heard of ninety-five of them. For the five entrepreneurs you have heard of, you have watched four of them go down fighting. There is only one person that made it. Hence, the 1 per cent left standing should have inspiring and appealing stories!

Statistics for thought

An article in 2018, from *Observer.com* shared that the top 3 per cent of YouTube channels had 90 per cent of total views, attracting on average 1.4 million views monthly. Even at that level, the average ad income is about $16,800 a year, less than one-third of the U.S. median household income.

This unfavourable success rate is not limited to the business world.

In sports, let's look at the NBA as an example. According to *Sportskeeda.com*, a study conducted by the NCAA in 2020, revealed that only 1.2 per cent of the collegiate players went on to play in the NBA.

The same goes for being on the big stage and silver screen. For people who want to make it big in the film industry, a study in 2019 by researchers from the Queen Mary University of London, using data from *Internet Movie Database* (IMDb) of the careers of over 2.3 million actors and actresses globally from 1888 found that only 2 per cent of actors make a living out of acting. It's important to note that making a living does not necessarily equate to making tons of millions as the A-listers we know, like the Angelina Jolies and Tom Cruises, who form an even tinier percentage.

Who's to say the ones who made it don't deserve to have inspiring stories?

You will undoubtably read or hear about some well-known enormous challenges and failures that these people deemed acceptable to be revealed to get to where they are. But you will never know the countless sacrifices, humiliating incidents, horrendous fights, damaging lawsuits, or the depth of the near-mental breakdowns they have experienced to come this far.

The 30th law

Make your accomplishments seem effortless—this is the 30th law in the book *The 48 Laws of Power* by Robert Greene, who also authored other books on strategy, power, and seduction. In the book, he mentioned that all the hard work, practice, and tricks employed must be concealed.

You must appear that you accomplished difficult feats effortlessly to inspire awe and admiration. If you expose how hard you worked and how much you suffered, it only makes you *mortal*. You want to convey to people that you have this exclusive gift that allows you to wield your powers at will, so you may continue to shroud yourself in an air of mystery to demonstrate your might and elicit reverence, so that people will see you as the person with the Midas touch.

Bringing it back to why successful people may want to make it look easy—many times, when these people share their knowledge, experiences, tips, or even try to lay out a framework for you, they intend to create their personal 'brand' and sell their stories and teachings through the persona of an idol whom people will follow. More often than not, they are selling dreams.

Of course, dreams can come true. But they are most likely supported by countless hours of *untold* hard work, which to be fair to the people who made it, sometimes is just too much for them to explain the overwhelming details.

> 'When you act, act effortlessly, as if you could do much more. Avoid the temptation of revealing how hard you work—it only raises questions.'
> —An excerpt from the book *The 48 Laws of Power*

The key lesson I wish to highlight is that *all that glitters is not gold*. Don't be bought into success stories and think you can be one of the protagonists without the required effort. I'm not saying that your journey will be filled with misery from start to end. I'm saying that success comes with battle scars. When you embark on your goal, be prepared for any rude awakening so the punch of reality doesn't throw you off.

Struggling does not mean failing

Without struggle, there is no progress. Struggle and discomfort are part of growth, and it can be intense, exhausting, frustrating, and simultaneously, deeply fulfilling.

This brings me back to my first panic attack. I woke up in fright one night with my heart thumping. My lungs were tightening, and I was gasping for breath. I was alone and terrified, and I started crying. I feared that I would lose control and have a heart attack. Thankfully, after twenty-but-felt-like-eternity minutes, I managed to calm down. Sadly, I never felt that my panic attack truly went away. The shadow of it lingered on. My anxiety didn't cease but merely lessened at times.

This attack happened during the period when I was in business school. I had paid a hefty tuition fee and depleted my savings, I was in a foreign land with limited cash, and I didn't know what would become of me in nine months. I expected an intense journey juggling studying, job seeking, and family, but I didn't anticipate the fear and anxiety. Why did I quit my stable and reasonably paid job to pursue an MBA? What if I ended up no better or worse than before?

I had stress rashes on my body every other day and regular breakouts on my face. To top it off, my hairdresser discovered two one-inch diameter bald spots on my scalp, which he attributed to stress.

In hindsight, I did have memorable and whimsical moments in business school. I paraglided at Chamonix-Mont-Blanc, watched Formula 1 in Sepang, Malaysia attended classes in costumes on INSEAD's traditional Dash Day, and studied with my group mates or practised for job interviews till the wee hours of the morning.

Those moments of joy, sweat, and bonding will remain with me forever. However, saying that 'It was a difficult period' will still be an understatement. The good news is that I reaped the rewards. I achieved what I wanted out of my experience in business school—making life-long friends and landing an incredible job, and I certainly felt an immense sense of pride and joy when I did it!

My study group and me in costumes during INSEAD's Dash Day

Struggle doesn't guarantee success but having it easy certainly won't

Phrases like 'change is painful' and 'struggles are part of growth' seem cliché because they are true. Nothing worth striving for comes easy. An easy path is always tempting, but it may be paved with red herrings that lead to unnecessary detours or back to the starting point. Going through certain gruelling phases en route to one's goals is often a reality unless you are extremely blessed.

I'm not suggesting that the right or only path to reach your goals is to put yourself through tremendous pressure or hardship. Choosing the hardest option does not always guarantee success. Sometimes you work hard; sometimes you work smart. The key takeaway is if you set your mind to do something, do it right, despite the hard work. As paradoxical as it sounds, it's possible to experience outer struggle and inner joy at the same time. If the struggle is an inevitable step of the transformation, and you emerge better and stronger by doing what is right, you will find harmony within yourself. It's part of your progress. It's part of your story.

'The wings of transformation are born of patience and struggle.'

—Janet S. Dickens

Come out of your transformation as the butterfly that flutters its fully-fledged wings and flies jovially.

"THOSE ARE MY PARENTS. AREN'T THEY TERRIFIC ?"

Key takeaways

- Serious effort is vital for success, and struggling is sometimes necessary for growth and transformation.
- Relying on familiar or easy methods can lead you down the wrong path or back to square one.
- Success stories are often carefully curated; the depth and breadth of struggles and failures that come with success are not always revealed.
- Sometimes we work hard; sometimes we work smart. The key is to choose to do it right and not fear and avoid hard work.

Chapter F

Friends Are the Family You Choose to Better You

'Families are the compass that guides us. They are the inspiration to reach great heights, and our comfort when we occasionally falter.'

—Brad Henry, former governor of Oklahoma

'A true friend is someone who thinks you are a good egg even though he knows you are slightly cracked.'

—Bernard Meltzer, late radio host of the advice call-in show *What's Your Problem?*

I once interviewed a Muay Thai fighter for a feature story more than a decade ago during my days as an editor. He told me that every time he won a big fight, he would receive plenty of congratulatory calls and messages. Once he lost badly, ended up in a hospital, and went jobless for months. Only his family and two close friends helped him through that period.

His story reminded me that there are no greater essentials than love and solidarity. Whom you have in your life through ups and downs matters. You may feel like you can take on the world alone because you have the means and capabilities, and I do not doubt that most of you can achieve what you set out to do. However, when times are laborious, you want to be able to count on family and friends. They offer support, security, and, very importantly, unconditional love. When times are luxurious, I hope you will appreciate the same people keeping you grounded and on your feet.

Forming new friendships

We may have a group of regular friends to hang out with, but it doesn't mean we can't make new friends. Popular TV shows like *Friends*, *How I Met Your Mother*, and *The Big Bang Theory* portray exclusive friendships, but reel life isn't real life, and sometimes real life dictates we make new friends, especially when you are living abroad. Some of you may not have the luxury of having your closest friends and family in proximity, but this doesn't mean you will stay alone unless you choose to. Being in a new environment is an opportunity to find new friends who may become your closest friends.

If you have just moved abroad, there are usually compatriot communities living in the same country and they will likely have experiences that you can relate to. There are also other people you can turn to, such as work mentors, colleagues, and even online communities who can offer advice or support in times of need.

No matter where you are based, at home or overseas, you can join associations such as civic groups, professional clubs, volunteer organizations, and preferably those that align with your interests or goals. You can socialize, work, or even travel with the members through volunteering activities, retreats, and projects. Through spending quality time together, you can know people on a deeper and broader level and form tighter bonds with the ones you clicked with.

While they are not immediate substitutes for your loved ones, these people can enrich your life in many ways. Often, you find role models who stimulate your motivation to become a better version of yourself. Some may eventually become your lifelong friends!

In my case, I wanted to improve my public speaking skills, so I visited a local Toastmasters club. I joined after the first meeting and never looked back! I love the energy and the diversity of the club's members—be it age, nationality, or profession. And I am in sync with its purpose—to help people become more confident in communicating, public speaking, and leading. The more senior members of the club provided great pointers that improved my pace, vocal variety, stage presence, and other aspects. I also had opportunities to lead. Within three months, I took on the role of a Sergeant-at-arms-someone who attends to guests, starts the meeting, introduces the agenda, and keeps order. After several years and leadership roles later, I eventually became the Club President!

In the blink of an eye, I have been a member for over fifteen years and have forged many firm friendships. I have collaborated with many of them, travelled with them, and competed with them, among other things. People with common interests or goals can assist you, motivate you, challenge your thinking, and help you stay accountable and steadfast to your goals. They can also watch out and caution you when any undesirable habit or behaviour becomes apparent. Maintaining quality friendships has a constructive impact on your well-being.

Be with the people you deserve

Real friends will not pull you down if they know you are trying to change for the better. If you need to reduce activities with friends to focus on your goal, such as studying for an exam or finishing a personal project, set the right expectations with them. Find alternatives to socialize. Prioritize quality over quantity when spending time. Don't be worried and think, 'My friends are going to ridicule or leave me if I don't join them!'

If your existing friends put you down or belittle you for pursuing a worthy cause instead of hanging out with them, maybe it's time to evaluate if you need new friends. Seeking personal growth does not make you better than your friends. It just puts you on a different path. If the common thing you have with them is the past, you have probably outgrown certain people, and that's normal. It's part and parcel of life as you go through different phases. Focus on friends who can evolve with you and your aspirations instead of those who hold you back.

'You are the average of the five people you spend the most time with.'

—Jim Rohn, entrepreneur, author, and
motivational speaker

Attitude is contagious. Be selective about who you hang out with. You may think that your friends do not dictate your actions, but they may influence what you think and ultimately choose to do. If you want to be successful, don't hang out with toxic people who infect you with their negative worldview, limiting mindset, complaining attitude, poor habits, and broken values. Associate with the type of people you want to become, who have the traits and achievements you desire, and learn from them. If their advice and suggestions don't resonate or work for you, then continue to experiment with other ones. If you have a clear goal in mind, you are more likely to achieve it by positioning yourself in the presence of motivating, uplifting, and optimistic people.

Friendships may even be developed through shared experience, but they are sustained through mutual respect and support. Surround yourself with people you trust, believe in you, and make you a better person.

If our family is the cake, then our friends are the icing. Together they make our lives sweeter.

Key takeaways

- Appreciate your family and real friends who will always be there for you through thick and thin.
- Making new friends through joining associations, clubs, and online communities that align with your interests and goals can add tremendous value to your life.
- Surround yourself with people who will make you a better person and avoid toxic influences. The people you hang out with will impact your personal growth and well-being.
- The right type of friends will support you, challenge you, and keep you motivated and accountable for your goals.

Chapter G

Give It Your Best Shot

'Do or do not. There is no try.'

—Yoda, legendary Jedi
Master of the *Star Wars* universe

I never forgot that girl. Sarah.

I met eight-year-old Sarah while helping at a centre for children with disabilities. Sarah had lost the use of her right and dominant hand and was practising with her left hand to do her homework. She dropped the pencil a few times, but picked it up each time and continued to write diligently. When I went up to her, she flashed the brightest smile and said, 'My handwriting is getting better.'

As I observed Sarah, I felt inspired and ashamed. Being a person with disabilities, Sarah had excuses not to do her homework or not to do anything, but she did and tried harder each time. Sarah gave it her best shot, every time.

Her fervent spirit hit me hard. It dawned on me that there were many instances in my life when I didn't embrace the opportunity or give my best shot because they required extra time, effort, or a detour. I chose to walk away or place myself on the side-line. For a split second, I gasped.

In this game of life, I had become a spectator, not a player.

Get on the playing field

This striking realization brought me back to the time when I used to play for my school basketball team. I hated it whenever an injury forced me to sit out for weeks, especially during competitions. During that period, I cheered for my team and even advised and mentored a couple of juniors. However, the unswerving truth stands,

Unless you're playing, you are not in the game.

There are three types of people. The first type gets in the game, the second type watches the game, and the third type wonders what the game is.

Get on the playing field. You can't wait for *the right moment* to take action. You make the *moment right*. Once you start doing it, you start learning. You discover insights, obtain feedback, and refine your approach to improve your game.

Sarah's can-do attitude struck a chord with me. I wanted to experience what life can bring when I get really engaged. I want to be in the heat of action, I want to make things happen, and I will give it my best shot!

What about you?

It takes courage to play. You need the nerves to walk the tightrope, knowing that you face victory's glory or defeat's ignominy. When you try your best, it can bring you wonders; it can also bring you disappointments. There are bound to be risks, trade-offs, and sacrifices, amid lots and lots and lots of hard work. However, you can't hope to get on to the medal podium by simply holding back and watching what happens.

The final 20 per cent matters

American actor and director Woody Allen once said, '80 per cent of success is showing up.'

While showing up is necessary, it's what you put in the final 20 per cent—the enthusiasm, the diligence, the charge—that makes all the meaningful difference to life because you went all the way. I prefer to say,

'100 per cent of living life lies in giving your best shot.'

Because of this, you are one step *closer* every day.

The final mile

Be it the final 20 per cent or 2 per cent, there's a saying that the last mile is always the hardest. The expression stems from a logistics context in which the last mile delivery of products from a warehouse to the destination i.e., the customer's doorsteps, is the most difficult and costly. With fewer deliveries in the final mile compared to earlier miles, the cost per delivery becomes higher, especially with more start–stops and minor or unfamiliar roads.

Yet, managing this last mile makes all the difference to the business and customer experience.

I remember this 'last mile' concept quite fondly. Back in school, my math teacher loved to give bonus questions on top of our regular homework. The good news is, since they are bonus questions, they are not mandatory. Most people in my class didn't bother to attempt those. I would *love* to be one of them. However, I also had a strict mother who ensured that I put in all the required effort to finish everything, down to the last bonus question. I've always resented her approach until a major exam when I realized that my math paper consists mostly of variations of the bonus questions, and I could answer them with relative ease!

In the end, I was one of the four students who scored more than 90 out of 100 points in a class of forty-three students. It felt pretty good!

As I reminisce this experience, what truly warms my heart, is not about coming up on top, it's about finally grasping the value of what putting the extra effort can add to your life.

Experience it for yourself. Get ready for your best shot.

Achieving your goals doesn't happen by chance. Play to win and give it your best shot. You never know what you get and whom you inspire.

Key takeaways

- If you wish to do something, don't hold back. Stop being a spectator and get on the playing field.
- There is no right moment to act; you make the moment right.
- Being in action is not enough; you need to give it your best shot. The additional effort you put in to give your best shot can make all the difference between doing and achieving.

Chapter H

Habits Maketh the Person

'Motivation is what gets you started. Habit is what keeps you going.'

—Jim Rohn, entrepreneur, author, and
motivational speaker

No one is certain how long it takes for a new habit to form. Some say twenty-one days, some say ninety days, and some say half a year. It depends on factors such as the type of habit, your personality, and circumstances, among many other things.

What's certain is that habits determine outcomes. While good habits produce positive outcomes, bad habits produce unwanted consequences. Hence, to reach your goals, you should identify your bad habits early and replace them with more productive ones to increase your likelihood of success.

While trying to form new habits, you may be tempted to slip back into your old ways. Don't be discouraged! Habit formation is a long-term process. You must give your mind and body time to adjust to a new routine. The good news is, our habits, once formed, become second nature. The key is to develop good habits to a point when they are in auto-pilot mode, so they become part of our unconscious behaviour and be eventually entrenched into our daily lives.

'Break an old pattern = Start a new habit.'

—Robin Sharma, leadership expert
and a writer best known for
The Monk Who Sold His Ferrari

Know why you are doing it

You must be clear on why you wish to adopt this habit and how it can help you achieve your goals. If you believe in its beneficial outcomes, you will be more motivated. Like setting a goal, it's effective to be specific with the habit you are trying to cultivate. In other words, if there are SMART goals, there should also be SMART habits. For example, instead of saying, 'I want to read more', say, 'I want to read one new self-help book a month to inspire me to stretch myself, do more, and be a better person.'

Another example is, instead of saying, 'I want to practise meditation', say, 'I want to practise meditation every morning to start my day with an inner sense of peace and balance.'

Identify the bad habits that block you

Bad habits produce undesirable outcomes. Before changing your bad habits, you need to know what they are. Some bad habits are pretty obvious. Still, because numerous habits are hardwired in most of our behaviours, it's not always clear to identify the ones that are causing you to be unproductive or those that result in negative consequences.

One approach is to research the bad habits typically associated with an area you wish to improve and see if any of your habits fit the description. Another approach is to ask people you are more comfortable with for feedback, especially if they have sufficient visibility on your routine.

Remember that most people, whether it's your family, friends, or colleagues, will not give you feedback voluntarily, especially on your bad habits! They don't want you to dislike them or hurt your feelings. Therefore, be sincere and let them know why you are doing so. It can be as simple as, 'I'm hoping to be more (something positive), but I can't seem to identify the actions or reasons that result in (negative consequence). I'd really appreciate it if you could let me know of any negative habits you may have observed, so I can take note and improve.'

It may be hard to hear the answers at first but remember the spirit and the intention behind it. Ask for specific examples or details if their answers don't register with you. Don't simply ignore the feedback. Otherwise, not only will you not improve and stay blind, but also push those people away. Be appreciative if they give feedback on what they think will help you despite risking your hostility and rebuttal. Thank them for being the messenger!

For a start, some of the less obvious bad habits in a range of endeavours include:

- Eating too quickly or too much at once.
- Not holding the door for someone just behind you.
- Making excuses.
- Spending too much time on your phone.
- Working too late into the night.
- Not finishing your sentences.
- Not looking at the person when you speak or when they speak to you.

Once you have identified your bad habits, you must identify what triggers them. This approach applies to your good habits too. Triggers help to create a method to stop or reduce your bad habits while developing and supporting your good habits.

Identify your triggers

X (Trigger) + Action = Y (Habit)

Triggers are crucial to forming new habits and breaking old ones. It can be anything that causes a habit to manifest.

- Have a cup of coffee (trigger), start work (habit).
- See posters of a fit model (trigger), exercise (habit).
- Talk to your boyfriend or girlfriend on the phone (trigger), sleep (habit).
- A sunny morning (trigger), go for a swim (habit).

- Finish a meal (trigger), smoke (habit).
- See a pastry shop (trigger), buy a cake (habit).
- Clean your desk (trigger), stop your work (habit).

Because X causes Y, identifying and understanding your triggers is the first step. If a trigger happens, the habit happens. If you wish to build or reinforce a habit, you activate the trigger. Likewise, if you wish to break a habit, you need to stop the trigger.

For example, if you want to cut down on refined sugar but there is a pastry shop two blocks away from your house, take a different route to avoid your trigger—seeing the pastry shop— so you prevent yourself from buying a cake. On the positive side, if you wish to be more active and your trigger to take a walk is an upbeat song, listen to these songs daily. The intention is to identify your triggers to develop good habits and strengthen their association, so those habits become automatic over time.

Don't add or change too many habits at once

Having a new goal and getting on to a new lifestyle is exciting. You're convinced of the benefits and want to nurture the good habits and overhaul the undesirable ones. But before you get carried away, be cautious that trying to change too many things at once may backfire on you.

For instance, let's assume your goal is to have $30,000 extra cash in one year for your own use. You take on a part-time job on top of your full-time job, cancel subscriptions and memberships, and cut your restaurant expenses. These new adjustments change many of your habits such as sleeping fewer hours daily, not going to the gym, and not dining out with friends. You risk not sustaining this routine because you are depriving and demanding a lot from your body and mind in a very short time.

A better approach is to prioritize or explore other options that allow for a more gradual shift. Work on changing the habits at an acceptable and sustainable pace.

Of course, if you are all geared up and have planned properly to set yourself up to achieve your goal under challenging circumstances, that is great news. Otherwise, select the former if you had to choose between achieving your goal at a slower rate and abandoning your goal because you are overwhelmed.

Remember, it's a marathon, not a sprint.

Seek support

In an earlier chapter, I spoke about the importance of support through family, friends, and peers. It does take a village to ensure that you get the needed support and establish a strong system to sustain your habits and achieve your goals. Reach out if you are facing difficulties or require support. It's not uncommon to delegate or relinquish certain responsibilities to fit new habits into your life while pursuing a new goal. For example, if you are studying part-time while working full-time and need to dedicate two hours daily to your studies, request your spouse or other family members to take care of matters at home.

I'm reminded of my friend Linda's remarkable story. Linda overhauled her hectic fourteen-hour-per-day-all-work-no-fun lifestyle after recovering from stage three breast cancer. With a renewed goal of wanting to live healthy and happily, she became a vegetarian, exercised every morning, worked no more than seven hours a day, and took vacations whenever she wished, all these while increasing her yearly net income to over $200,000! How did she achieve this? You probably guessed it. Support.

Linda was a one-woman show as a real estate agent. She had to arrange appointments, follow up on leads, meet clients, prepare paperwork, maintain and update listings, market her properties, research the market, and so on. Of all the responsibilities, Linda enjoys selling and servicing clients the most. Her other work, however, bogged her down, leaving her unhappy, exhausted, stressed, and ultimately sick.

After her cancer ordeal, Linda realized that life was too short. Under the advice of her friends and family, she was finally convinced and resigned to reduce her income by forking out part of her commission to hire a personal assistant. Little did Linda know that she would get more clients and close more deals! With her assistant Min Min helping her with the time-consuming tasks she disliked, Linda could focus her energy on networking, client servicing, and sales. She ended up getting more clients and closing more deals. With every deal closed, she gave Min Min a percentage of her commission as a bonus to encourage her efforts.

What a win-win situation! Linda makes more money than before even though she is working less. Most importantly, she is living a healthier and happier life.

Don't fall into the habit of trying to fix or do everything yourself. There is no shame in letting people know that you need help. Not only can family, friends, coaches, or mentors help and encourage you, but also keep you accountable. It's acceptable and logical to leverage all the support and resources you can get as long as you are not taking advantage of anyone for selfish gains.

Endure the beginning

The most critical and hardest phase lies in the beginning. This phase can last a week, a month, or longer. It's also a phase where you are committed to programming yourself and overriding your default behaviour to establish a new one. There are three techniques that I have learnt and used that may help you to stick to a new habit.

(i) Habit stacking

Habit stacking is adding a new habit by combining it with an existing one. The term as formulated by S.J. Scott in his book *Habit Stacking: 97 Small Life Changes That Take Five Minutes or Less*. Introducing a new habit to what you are already doing makes it easier to embed the new habit. Let me share how I apply this technique to my situation. I have to carve out fifteen minutes daily to strengthen my core muscles through a series of exercises as advised by my physiotherapist. I detest the thought of doing them, but they are necessary due to an old injury in my lower back. To ensure I keep to this new habit, I *stack* them on top of my daily workout. Now, after every workout, I will focus on my core muscles. I don't feel complete without my core exercises!

(ii) Temptation bundling

The term temptation bundling was invented by Katherine Milkman, behavioural economist and professor at the Wharton School at the University of Pennsylvania. The concept behind this is that you bundle or pair an activity you like that brings you pleasure with an activity you don't like to do but is necessary. Hence, you'll be more motivated to do the harder task if you can also do something you like along with it or after it. For example, there are people who go to the gym if they could also use this time to watch their favourite drama. I treat myself to a lovely full-body massage only after I complete my monthly household duties. Think about the habits you wish to develop and how you want to apply this technique to your life.

(iii) Plan broad and detailed

Thanks to my job in programme managing, I've been trained to be detailed in planning which has served me well in my everyday life. I check and plan my schedule for the upcoming week at the end of every Friday and then have detailed planning for each specific day the evening before. This practice is an excellent method to push yourself to think through your time and incorporate the new habits that you need to develop into your schedule as part of your goals. Planning for the upcoming week at the end of Fridays serves three purposes.

Firstly, I have an overview of key appointments and meetings, personally and professionally, to assess how heavy or light the upcoming week is so I can prime myself. Secondly, I have enough time to react or adjust plans since I can use the weekends to sort out matters. Thirdly, planning for the upcoming week at the end of Fridays also sends a mental signal that I'm closing my work week. Think of it as a shutdown ritual.

As for the detailed planning every evening, I will check my calendar for the latest meetings I have the following day. Then I will spend about ten minutes writing a to-do list whereby I schedule tasks into various timeslots for every hour of the day, including time for buffers, lunch, and exercises. This practice also applies to weekends, especially if I have commitments, although I tend to set aside more free time than workdays. Feel free to use this method to plan time for leisure activities and hobbies too!

You may wonder, what about times when I have to entertain last-minute requests or meetings? In my view, this makes planning even more important! I can look at my already planned schedule and quickly assess how to reshuffle my priorities, postpone some tasks, or simply say no. (You will read more about this in Chapter N.) Planning to a tee need not be rigid and strict. In fact, writing down what I have to do gives me a sense of relief and comfort. In Chapter A, I mentioned that transferring floating thoughts on to paper frees you of the responsibility to remember them and declutters the mind.

As a result of this habit, I sleep better at night because I don't have to keep thinking about what I need to do the next day. Just as importantly, I don't have to spend extra time and energy in the morning thinking about my day and what I need to do first. Planning the night in advance takes me right into work mode the next day. Similarly, planning for items and activities associated with your habits the night before takes you right into the habit the next day!

Persevere with the habits daily. It will become part of your routine once you make it through this phase.

Persist, persist, persist, and follow through.

Good habits are the fundamental building blocks of success. Make those habits, and the habits will make you.

Key takeaways

- Habits determine outcomes. Replacing bad habits with productive ones increases the likelihood of success.
- Understanding how a habit enables your goals helps keep you motivated. Be specific about the habits you wish to cultivate. The SMART acronym can be applied to habits.
- Identify your bad habits and the triggers behind those habits. Stopping the triggers is one way to stop the bad habits. The same logic applies to cultivating good habits.
- Avoid changing too many habits at once. Stay focused and seek support when needed to sustain the momentum.
- Techniques to help you incorporate and stick to the new habits include habit stacking, temptation bundling, and detailed planning.

Chapter I
Invest in Yourself

'The best investment you can make is an investment in yourself. The more you learn, the more you'll earn.'
—Warren Buffet, business magnate, investor, and philanthropist

You need to give something to get something. Without inputs, there is no output.

I have three rules when it comes to investment:

- Invest as early as possible.
- Invest in personal development.
- Invest in what is most suitable for you.

Time is your best capital, so you should invest as early as possible. Investment can increase in value over the years, and generally, the earlier you invest, the more time your investment has to grow.

What I refer to as investment need not be limited to bonds, stocks, insurance, or other financial types of products, which I am all for investing in as they increase in value over time and provide payment. More specifically, I wish to point out that investment in education follows the same logic. Education is a lifelong currency. The sooner you embark on it, the more knowledge and skills you acquire and the more value you offer. You reap the benefits because your personal value appreciates.

I'm not shy to admit that one of my goals was to land a desirable job and make more money. For that to happen, broadening my skills, knowledge, and opportunities was important, so I decided to invest in a Master of Business Administration (MBA). Of course, you don't need to go through the MBA route to make more money. There are numerous ways to invest in yourself. I just chose what I felt would work best for me. Indeed, my experience at INSEAD opened multiple doors.

Despite all the hard work and stress I had to bear, pursuing my MBA was my best professional decision to increase my value.

Applying the philosophy of Kaizen to yourself

Just before entering business school, I worked in a Japanese multinational company and was influenced by 'Kaizen'. Originating in Japan, 'Kaizen' translates to 'change for the better'. It's a business philosophy that emphasizes continuous improvements across all operations, applies to all employees, from the CEO to the assembly line, and is adopted by many companies globally. It involves making gradual, improved, and sustained changes to activities and processes to increase efficiency and reduce waste. Kaizen is embedded in the way of business and the mindset of its employees. Traditionally applied to manufacturing processes, the philosophy has permeated and been adopted in many aspects of life, such as health, wealth, and relationships.

I find applying Kaizen to my personal life to be tremendously effective. A year ago, I wanted to feel more energized in the morning, so I started by forcing myself to wake up an hour earlier to exercise. I stopped after barely one week! I thought I'd get more accomplished by having an extra hour in the morning but that wasn't sustainable. Instead, I began by waking up just ten minutes earlier, and I would immediately step out to get some sun to wake myself up and do basic stretches. Gradually, ten minutes became fifteen, then twenty. Today, I wake up forty-five minutes earlier and get my body moving, whether walking or swimming, to start the day. Getting to your goal doesn't always involve taking a big leap; many small gradual steps can get you there.

Tip: If that still doesn't refresh you, get into a cold shower! It will increase your dopamine and alertness.

If the only constant in this world is change, it makes sense that we have to continuously improve ourselves to keep up with opportunities, challenges, and demands that come with change. Making the right investment in ourselves, whether it's to pick up a new technical competency, improve our relationship management skills, or increase our mental and physical fitness, is extremely vital to stay relevant.

Focus on what you can enable from within you

You must be wondering at this point if all investments cost money! That is not true. Some investments don't require capital. It's not always about spending money to get more financial returns. Spending time and effort to improve yourself or the things that matter to you is a fantastic form of non-monetary investment. Depending on your goals and what you are trying to achieve, decide what method is most suitable for you.

For example, you intend to live healthier, so you try quitting smoking. You want dinner to be the time and place to connect with family over good food and ambiance, so you pick up online cooking tips and set up the dining space. You aim to be more productive, so you revamp your sleep habits to wake up early to feel energized. All these efforts contribute to your personal development, well-being, and the lives of those around you, without needing money. Money is not a prerequisite to improving and investing in yourself. You'll be surprised at the changes you can make without it.

Focus on the payoff, not the payment

Although there are goals that can be achieved without money, there are also goals that you can achieve in an accelerated manner if you make the appropriate monetary investments.

It's often about finding the optimal mix of your ambition, time, effort, and willingness to pay.

If you wish to learn a new language, you may consider enrolling in classes. You can choose to self-learn, but that process will take a lot longer than having a teacher guide you through the grammar, communicate with you in the language, practice, and learn with others. Being in the classroom with other students creates an immersive experience that will expedite your learning process.

On the same note, it's probably worth considering getting a coach if you wish to pick up a sport such as tennis, golf, or even swimming. A coach will facilitate your development by guiding you on the movement and techniques, and, more importantly, minimizing the injury risk that hinders your progress. Don't hesitate. Investing in yourself is the best form of return.

You are your greatest asset, and you're worth every sweat and every penny.

Key takeaways

- My three rules of investing: Invest as early as possible; sound investment is likely to appreciate over time. Invest in personal development and invest in what's most suitable for you.
- Continuous improvement is key to keeping up with opportunities, challenges, and demands in a world that is ever-changing.
- Investment does not always require money. You can invest time and effort to improve yourself, your relationships, your well-being, and the lives of people who matter to you.
- If you must make monetary investments, focus on the payoff, not the payment. Remember, value is greater than cost.

Chapter J
Jazz It Up!

'I add chilli to almost every meal. It jazzes up my tongue, my brain, my spine, and every cell in my body.'

—Yours truly

Imagine walking into an apartment with white walls, white furniture, and white tiles, it's rather uninspiring, isn't it? It makes you feel . . . lifeless.

You don't want to feel this way in your journey to achieving your goals. You want to feel a kaleidoscope of emotions—it can be excitement, fear, relief, or discomfort, but you must feel something beyond a flatline.

Getting bored can happen quickly and surrendering your goals to boredom is a real possibility. To prevent boredom from setting in, you need to jazz up your journey by sprinkling elements that spark joy, excitement, and intensity, so your journey will not be insipid. You will feel more stimulated, engaged, and connected with your goals.

'Do anything, but let it produce joy.'

—Walt Whitman, one of the most influential poets in the American literature

Inject variety

Variety benefits us in many ways—the richness of the diverse experiences and the thrill of novelty. A common case I hear from my peers is, 'I strongly believe being a vegetarian is good for my health and the planet, but I can't imagine just having eggs, beans, and mushrooms as proteins.' If you want to become a vegetarian, the meal (and protein) options are abundant! There are many cuisines with delicious vegetarian recipes and different methods of preparing food. Having a meatless diet need not be bland. To get more ideas or inspiration, you can treat yourself to lovely vegetarian restaurants, watch cooking shows, or attend vegetarian cooking classes. Allow your imagination to be stretched. You'll be amazed at how diverse and comprehensive your menu can be!

To make 'injecting variety' not become another predictable pattern is to embrace a new experience sufficiently. Let it sink in before moving on to another. Strike a balance between current focus and new exploration.

Join a competition

Competitions are opportunities to challenge yourself, step up your gear, and bring out your fullest potential. You will learn tremendously by participating in one, be it your strengths and weaknesses, your current limits, your ability to handle pressure, your skills in problem-solving, collaboration, and many more!

Take this, for example. Suppose your desire is to become much stronger, and you want to build muscles but find weightlifting in the gym repetitive and unmotivating. In that case you can boost your enthusiasm by joining an iron-man competition. That'll get your juices pumping now that you are lifting weights for a reason! You'll be more dedicated, focused on your goal, and look for ways to improve your performance.

Competition brings me back to my experiences in public speaking competitions. As I mentioned in Chapter F, I joined a public speaking club, Toastmasters, where members are encouraged to take on various roles to hone their communications and presentation skills through delivering prepared and impromptu speeches and evaluations. Toastmasters International has a yearly competition in which participants will first compete at a club level before moving through several levels until the final.

Before I joined the competitions, I was already delivering speeches to a crowd of 50–80. But competing just sets everything in a different sphere. I can't put into words the amount and depth of concentration and dedication I put into crafting a speech, rehearsing, and eventually delivering it. The emotions along the process were like someone had poured chilli, lime, honey, and bitter melon down my throat and blended them in my stomach. You get all the feelings at once when someone pushes the blending button and have various flavours show up. Those feelings were palpable, and I vividly remembered certain moments and emotions.

The *massive gratitude* when some mentors took the time to coach and improve my stage presence, body movements, and other techniques to help me through various rounds: The margin between a winner and a runner-up was so slight that I appreciated every advice to improve my speech content and delivery.

The *extreme nervousness* as I entered the competition arena: I arrived an hour earlier to settle myself for the competition, and I remembered my legs not coordinating as I walked up the stairs. When people greeted me, I replied in a trembling and broken voice. My stomach was churning, my body was heating up, my face was red, and I broke up in cold sweat for the first time. Public speaking is scary enough, and being in a public speaking competition was far more hair-raising than when I attempted bungee jumping.

The *immense joy and pride* that lasted for days when my name was announced as the winner: I didn't eventually make it to the global stage, but the fact that I beat two past national champions was a feat to remember.

This competition transformed me. It upped my game! I benefited tremendously through learning about myself and from other contestants and mentors. Every time I competed, I felt that I had expanded my limits, my mental toughness, my ability to handle pressure, my character development, and my range of skills in public speaking.

Go for it! Join a competition! Experience the kaleidoscope of emotions that competitions can bring.

Have a theme

It's fun to incorporate themes occasionally to make pursuing your goals memorable. If your goal is to spend more time with your family instead of relaxing aimlessly, you can organize a Lego day where you visit Legoland, build things using Lego bricks, and watch a Lego movie. No Legoland in your city? No problem. You can have a nature day where you hike in the forest, picnic, or camp overnight. Depending on the available options, you can have science day, art-and-craft day, animals day, or cooking day. The list goes on.

Blitz days

When I was working with sales teams, I participated in Blitz Days which were organized occasionally. Different companies have slight variations in terms of how they run Blitz Day. In a nutshell, Blitz Day is a day on which employees from one or several departments are fully focused on one objective, such as calling existing customers to get them to sign on to a new package or cold calling individuals in their database to generate leads. There will be a surge in the particular activity to try and obtain the targets set for Blitz Day. The common elements are that it's a team activity, it takes place over a short period, usually no more than a day, and there will be prizes to make it competitive and exciting.

Why not plan occasional Blitz Days in your goal journey? If you are already running a business and your goals are to increase your revenue or client base by 50 per cent or more, you can organize a Blitz Day to get your employees fired up. If you and your peers are trying to tidy your homes and declutter, organize a Blitz Day together. The person who packed the most boxes of clothes, books, and household items ready to be donated or discarded by the end of the day wins. Although having a team is a common element in Blitz Day, if you are alone, you can create a Blitz Day where you focus intensely on one activity that will contribute towards your goal.

A Blitz Day is just one example of a focus day employed by sales teams. There are also hackathons that bring computer programmers, engineers, and interface designers together to collaborate in building or improving a new software or hardware over a short period, typically twenty-four to forty-eight hours. The idea is to make the day intense, fun, and productive.

Challenge yourself to do something absurd or extremely out of your comfort zone

Challenging yourself or accepting challenges bursts wide open the box of what is possible. Through stepping into a challenge or a new zone, you unveil new experiences, perspectives, and realities and have you looking more profoundly into yourself to foster deeper learning.

I had a client who believed she couldn't make friends because she was an introvert. I challenged her to go to a networking event, socialize, and obtain name cards of at least thirty people. In the end, she made a new friend who shared her hobby of candle-making. Through that experience, she realized that she is actually adept at making friends. It's a matter of finding people with the same interests.

Let's expand on the above example.

If you tend to feel awkward in social situations and aim to be less shy, force yourself to strike up conversations with strangers. It can be as simple as saying hi to the people you meet in the lift and casually asking how they are. To kick it up a notch, you can join social clubs and meet people likely to share certain interests and engage in longer conversations. To be even more extreme and put yourself out there, join speed dating events, even if you are not looking for a potential partner!

The structure of speed dating enables you to meet many people face-to-face within a specific session. You are given just enough time to form an initial impression of those people, evaluate if you want to meet them again and spend more time forging a better understanding. The purpose here is not to find you a prospective partner, but to get you to speak to as many people as possible to get you out of your comfort zone, confront your fear, and gain newfound perspectives through such interactions.

One or more of the above suggestions may sound preposterous to a shy and socially awkward person. But be it any goal, getting out of your comfort zone brings enormous benefits. You may be able to go further than you thought, realize that it's not as frightening as you assumed, and discover something that you actually appreciate. More importantly, you feel proud that you've done it. It can be overwhelming at first, but after you have tried it once, you may be tempted to do so again as you are more confident to face similar situations after stretching your limits.

Who knew?

'Don't forget: Temporary insanity moments spice up your life.'
—Paulo Coelho, lyricist and novelist best known
for his novel *The Alchemist*

Jazz it up!

Key takeaways

- Jazz up your journey to keep the process interesting so you feel more stimulated, engaged, and connected with your goals.
- Injecting variety, joining competitions, organizing 'theme' days, and embracing new and challenging activities are ideas to spice up your journey and your life!

Chapter K

Kindness, Especially to Yourself, Goes a Long Way

'You only have peace when you make it with yourself.'
—Mitch Albom, musician, journalist,
and author of one of my favourite books,
Tuesdays with Morrie

How often do you judge yourself? How often do you berate yourself or prematurely conclude that you suck?

While a healthy dose of self-evaluation helps you to reflect and improve yourself, being too self-critical leaves you feeling insecure and incompetent. Dwelling on negativities can have a spiralling effect that causes anxiety, fear of failure, lack of motivation, and productivity, thus eventually derailing you from your goals. That is not the outcome you want.

We are guilty of judging ourselves from time to time, but too much of it traps us in a loop and puts us in danger of becoming our own bullies. Let's look at some key signs.

You want to be ahead, and you fear losing your edge

You believe being tough on yourself helps you achieve more or perform better. In fact, many of us are taught this belief from a young age. As a child, I heard enough phrases and stories from my parents and teachers about, 'No pain no gain' and, 'If you are not being tough on yourself, you are not going anywhere'. Subconsciously, many of us hold entrenched assumptions about the need to be hard on ourselves so we don't turn into lazy, unproductive, or worthless people. What's important to understand here is that correlation does not imply causation. Being overly harsh on yourself is not a prerequisite or a necessity to be ahead or be successful.

You feel that you didn't measure up to your own expectations of achievement

The truth is, when it comes to the desire to achieve something, it'll never be enough. You think you'll be happy when you achieve X, but once you have it, you will want to achieve Y. You may argue that the sky's the limit, and yet a billionaire like Elon Musk already has his sights set beyond our skies with his goal of a crewed mission to Mars by the end of the decade! Nothing will ever be enough. Instead of being preoccupied with what's next, indulge in the present and appreciate what you have.

You constantly compare yourself to others and fixate on what you don't have

One time, during an important annual national examination, I didn't perform well and failed to make it to my desired junior college. My mother came down hard on me. 'Why can't you be as good as your classmate Mei Yin? She has straight As!' (By the way, this is a sanitized version.) For years, I was jealous of Mei Yin's achievements. She wasn't only a straight-A student, but also the president of the Guitar Club. 'Her mother must be so proud', I thought sarcastically. I did not realize until much later that Mei Yin lost her mother at the age of eight.

That discovery changed my perspective. Unless you know every single detail of the life of the person you're comparing yourself to, there is no need to be needlessly envious. There's always someone who has what you don't have, and vice versa.

You become excessively concerned about what people think of you

Let me save you some agony—no one cares! No one really cares the way you think they do. For example, when you make a blunder during a meeting, do you tend to panic and kick yourself for hours or days, 'Oh no, people must be talking about how stupid I am!'

If you feel that you are being made the topic of discussion, you fall prey to the spotlight effect—a term created by psychologists Thomas Gilovich, Victoria Husted Medvec, and Kenneth Savitsky to describe a phenomenon where people tend to overestimate how much they are being noticed for their flaws or mistakes as if they are put under a spotlight. The next time you catch yourself overthinking, stop! Reframe your mindset to 'People might have noticed my blunder, but it's not worth their time talking about it.' You have greater things ahead that are more worthy of your attention.

You use self- judgement as a coping mechanism, consciously or unconsciously

If you are your harshest critic, you won't feel as affected when people judge you because you have cushioned that impact, ironically, through your self-judgement. I'm guilty of employing this method in the past. Every time I have my work performance review meeting with my manager, I judge myself critically to prepare for all types of onslaughts. I have always felt that if I were to deal myself the hardest slap, I would be able to endure all the others.

Don't feel ashamed if any of the above signs resonate with you. You are just trying to be a better version of yourself. However, we need to be mindful of the effects of insidious chronic self-judgement. It's through understanding why we subject ourselves to it and what's keeping us there that we can learn to resist and let it go.

Cut yourself some slack

Realize it's time for a change. Self-judgement will not serve additional benefits beyond its initial value to improve ourselves through adequate evaluation and reflection. Self-compassion is proven to lead to greater achievement than self-criticism ever could. Why not try seeing yourself from a kinder view and allow yourself some approval and tenderness?

'I work 12 hours a day, I exercise 7 days a week, I prepare healthy meals at home instead of going out and it's all paying off. I'm finally too tired to care about being perfect!'

©Glasbergen / glasbergen.com

Accept that everyone is different and that you are enough

We begin at different points in life, and there is no way to compare objectively and fairly. Honour your qualities. Respect and value yourself for who you are and what you have accomplished.

Look for your inner ally

We all have our inner critics. Now it's time to meet our inner ally. Have the support, understanding, and care for yourself as you would with a good friend. Access your internal pool of compassion and present that to yourself. Self-compassion allows for greater self-love and is a strong nurturing and motivating force to achieve wholeness and well-being.

Forgive your mistakes

Like complaining, constantly blaming yourself only traps you in misery and frustration and will not improve things. Recognize that making mistakes is part and parcel of life. Your attitude towards handling your mistakes is more critical than your mistakes per se. Therefore, acknowledge your mistakes, learn from the experiences, and resolve to improve.

Shift your perspectives on success and perfection

As long as you are constantly doing something to improve yourself or the lives of people around you, you are productive and capable. Wanting to achieve is commendable; wanting to overachieve at the expense of yourself is criminal.

Take care of your health

Caring for yourself includes getting sufficient sleep, not skipping meals, and doing activities that release stress and improve your physical, mental, and emotional well-being. Carve out time and space to decompress and recharge. If we feel healthy, we tend to be happier and see things from a more optimistic perspective.

'If your compassion does not include yourself, it's incomplete.'
—Jack Kornfield, author of *A Path with Heart* and
a teacher of mindfulness meditation worldwide

If you haven't accepted your humanness, it's time to reset your view. Kindness goes a long way. Be kind to yourself, and then be kind to others.

Judge less, love more. You'll be amazed at who you see in the mirror.

Always remember,

Kindness = 1/Judgement.

Key takeaways

- Being too self-critical may cause negative effects, such as insecurity, fear of failure, and lack of motivation, and derail you from your goals.
- Don't allow yourself to be your own bully by being overly harsh, having insatiable expectations of achievements, comparing constantly with people, and fixating on people's opinions.
- Self-compassion leads to greater achievement than self-criticism ever could.
- Accepting yourself, forgiving your mistakes, looking for your inner ally, resetting your perspectives, and taking care of yourself are crucial to developing self-compassion.

Chapter L

Learn from Both Failures and Successes

'Success is a learnable skill. You can learn to succeed at anything.'
—T. Harv Eker, businessperson, motivational speaker, and author known for his theories on wealth and motivation

'The only real mistake is the one from which we learn nothing.'
—Henry Ford, industrialist, business magnate, and founder of the Ford Motor Company

Tell me if the following sounds familiar.

'You must learn from your failure!'
'You must learn from your mistakes!'

I've heard the above many times from my parents, teachers, and mentors, and I agree. I should. We all should. Mistakes and failures are an integral part of the learning process or success process. Emerging from failures successfully builds resilience, new knowledge, and enlightened perspectives. However, while learning from failures is vital, learning from successes is just as essential and effective.

Would you learn to cook from the failed recipes of others?

Time matters. We want to learn what works in the shortest time.

If you learn from failures, you learn what didn't work but didn't learn what would work. Maybe you won't make the same mistake twice, but that doesn't prevent you from making a different mistake. Additionally, focusing too much on failures, even if it's the failures of others, can be detrimental to your self-confidence in the long run.

If you learn from success, at least you know that something can and has worked for you or the person in that situation. If you were involved in the process, you would know what was done right, why it worked, and focus on how you can repeat the success. Building a repertoire of best practices is critical.

More efficiently, you don't have to start on a blank page and figure from scratch. You can draw parallels, be it from the success of others, and extrapolate applicable elements to your situations or draw parallels from your successes to enhance your current situation or apply them to a new situation. You have a higher chance of continuing success and making what has worked even better by studying successes than failures.

What your brain says

Neuroscientist Earl Miller from the Massachusetts Institute of Technology led research that found that success influences the brain more strongly than failure through improving neural processing. Neurons in the brain can remember recent successes and failures during learning and perform better after doing it right than after doing it wrong.

In Miller's study that involved observing monkeys, he discovered that the neurons in their brains responded differently following correct and incorrect responses, with correct responses setting up the brain for additional successes. After a wrong response, he observed that there was less neural activity and no improvement in further attempts. By understanding the brains of humans and animals, which are identical in these fundamental functions, Miller believes he can apply the findings to many aspects of our daily lives.

Before you go on, I wish to emphasize - *don't* diss learning from failures.

This chapter is not about learning only from success, it's about *not neglecting* to learn from successes.

Taking personal responsibility to learn from the failures and successes of yourself and others to achieve greater goals is a goal in itself. No matter the stage or state of your journey, you can learn from timeless tips.

(i) Read, research, and network widely

Some books, articles, and podcasts discuss what worked and what didn't, as well as insights and analyses on the latest trends or projections in your chosen area. Join groups, tap your alumni network, and leverage social media to find or ask to be introduced to people who have been in your shoes or are taking the paths you desire. Learn why they chose this journey, what they went through, what contributed to positive outcomes, what pitfalls to avoid, and how they dealt with various situations. You will be more prepared mentally and richer knowledge-wise.

(ii) If you experience success, stay humble and grounded

Evaluate your struggles, take stock of the actions and methods that worked, and appreciate the people who have stimulated and walked with you. Success is not permanent; hence it's important not to stop questioning and reflect on how you arrived at each victory, each milestone, and the feedback received during the journey. They are crucial to continuing your success or attempting other goals.

(iii)　If things haven't gone your way, take some time to recover and assess what happened

Was this outcome preventable, or did unexpected circumstances cause this? Did you make an erroneous decision, trust the wrong people, need more suitable tools, and so on? It could also be a combination of multiple factors. Do a retrospect and dissect the situation: review your records such as proposals, diaries, and conversations. Sometimes, you can't avoid asking yourself hard questions. To provide a more objective assessment, bring a third party who knows the situation but is not palpably involved.

> Learn from those before you. Recognize successes and evaluate achievements. Acknowledge failures and assess inadequacies.

Fail and figure out

Failures aren't necessarily all bleak; this is a neglected perspective. Every experience teaches you something valuable. If you are devising formulas, learning a new skill, writing a book, or designing a product, it's not uncommon to not succeed at first.

We often hear the term 'trial and error'. It's a problem-solving method in which you experiment continuously with various approaches to doing something, analyse, and change until you find the most successful one.

When I was working in an innovation lab, we centred on building proofs-of-concept, or POC for short. A POC demonstrates that an idea has the potential for real-world application with a minimum viable product. Our approach to building POC is called 'Agile'; the trial-and-error method is a key component of Agile. It encourages risk-taking, making mistakes, learning, and then adjusting quickly. Building POC is critical because it de-risks the execution of the project by allowing companies to invest minimally to test the idea's viability with customers and validate that it makes sense before going all out to build a complete version.

In such cases, one is prepared to make many small tries and learn from them before making a substantial investment or a longer-term commitment.

Trial-and-error is not exclusive to business or innovation-related activities. There are many real-world examples of them. You are likely to have encountered at least one of them.

- Participating in various social activities before joining a club.
- Dating different people before finding the one whom you would like to spend your life with.
- Experimenting with different fitness routines before finding one that works best for you.
- Playing with different mice for gaming before determining one that optimizes your performance.
- Using various types of moisturizers before deciding which is most suitable for your skin.
- Dining at various restaurants before choosing one to host your birthday party.
- Trying out spas at different places before signing a package with one.

In a capricious world, successes and failures are ephemeral. As financier and CEO of Blackhawk Partners Inc Ziad

Abdelnour said, 'Never let success get to your head and never let failure get to your heart.'

There is no end to learning.

'Stay hungry. stay foolish.'

—Steve Jobs, co-founder of Apple

Key takeaways

- It's essential to learn from both failures and successes to achieve greater goals.
- Learning from successes allows you to build a repertoire of best practices and draw parallels to enhance your current situation or apply them to a new situation.
- Learning from failures builds new knowledge and perspectives. Trial-and-error encourages people to experiment continuously with various approaches to doing something, analyse, and change until they find the most successful one.

Chapter M
Maintain
Momentum

'Keep moving ahead because action creates momentum, which in turn creates unanticipated opportunities.'
—Nick Vujicic, world renowned speaker
who has tetra-amelia syndrome,
a disorder characterised by the
absence of arms and legs.

There are countless tasks to finish before you reach your goals. The hardest thing about a task is to start. The second hardest? The chapter title says it all. Maintaining momentum to the finish point is as difficult as beginning the action. Don't fret; there are ways to help you stay in motion.

Start small and simple

You can be bold with your end goal, but you can also start small and simple.

In Chapter A, I mentioned taking the path of least resistance if you find it difficult to reach your goals. It applies here too, especially in the beginning. Don't confuse it with not being bold. As Chinese philosopher Confucius said, 'The man who moves a mountain begins by carrying away small stones', you can reach your bold goals by starting small and simple. It's easier to accomplish a daily twenty-minute walk than a weekly two-hour hike. It's easier to reduce your cigarettes stick by stick than to go cold turkey.

When you break things down into smaller pieces or tasks, you make them clearer, easier to digest, and less daunting. You minimize the resistance, doubt, or agony that accompanies it. Breaking things down helps you to avoid stress and procrastination. You feel more assured and motivated to move from one task to another. You can pick up the pace once you get it into your routine, make it a habit, and pass the 'flight risk' phase.

Practice, practice, practice

Have you tried to swim successfully by watching hours of YouTube videos or flapping your arms and legs on a yoga mat? If you did, I'd like to learn the secret! To get to where you want, it's about real practice.

When I participate in public speaking competitions, I rehearse my speech, typically about seven minutes long, thirty-five to forty times across three stages. I thought that was enough. In reality, that was nothing. A fellow public speaker, I will call him Charles since he doesn't wish to be named, who is known for his humorous speeches, was crowned champion four times, and the first runner-up three times at Toastmasters International District level competition, revealed that he had practised his speech around 500 times in the run-up to the championships! That is 3,500 minutes or more than fifty-eight hours!

To be good at something takes time. To be excellent takes a much, much longer time. It doesn't happen overnight. The truth is, we are spoilt in our expectations of things. Be it getting fast answers online or overnight delivery or video on demand, we are so used to instant gratification that having to spend hours practising, refining, and practising speeches, in this example, is so unenticing that we are tempted to stop our advances. There is only one universal rule to achieving mastery commit time every day to work at it.

The margin of greatness contains uncountable hours of hard work.

Practice leads to progress and mastery, if you do it right

Here's an important distinction. You have to practise it right! If you spend days, weeks, and months practising the wrong thing, you won't make any progress; you may even regress. Make sure you get the techniques, tools, materials, or whatever is needed. Consider seeking the help of a coach, trainer, or mentor to guide you properly.

Practise it often. Practise it right. When you get better, the momentum gets easier.

Simplify your life

Simplicity brings clarity. Yet, there are many reasons why we don't head towards simplicity.

It may be due to external influence or internal assumptions, but many of us tend to feel that the things worth striving for should be difficult. As a result, we tend to over-complicate things. However, there's also a tendency to brag about the complexity of the things we attempt. It's part of showmanship or to get attention, trying to portray our goal as Herculean to earn the awe of people and the need to feel like we matter. And these reasons are just off the top of my head!

Even the famous American author, Mark Twain, said, 'I've had a lot of worries in my life, most of which never happened.'

Overthinking derails momentum if people choose to dwell in complication. It creates anxiety, inaction, and a string of unintended consequences. The truth is, there is more sophistication in simplicity. Keeping it simple allows you to focus better and consistently work towards your goal, thus generating and maintaining momentum.

Steve Jobs said, 'That is been one of my mantras—focus and simplicity. Simple can be harder than complex. You have to work hard to get your thinking clean to make it simple. But it's worth it in the end because once you get there, you can move mountains.'

'Keep it fast, keep it fair, keep it simple. That's our motto
here at the law firm of Rock, Paper and Scissors.'

© Glasbergen/ glasbergen.com

Celebrate, just celebrate

Many people I know don't celebrate enough for pretty much
the same reason—is it worth celebrating?

Yes, and yes, it is! Celebration is key to sustaining
productivity, morale, and momentum! People don't celebrate
enough because they want to reserve celebrations for massive
achievements. However, if you set your sights on only the grand
moments, you're short-changing yourself and perhaps others.

Celebrations don't always mean throwing mega parties and
announcing to the world that you've achieved a monumental
milestone. It can be as simple as saying 'Thank You' to show
gratitude and appreciation for your present situation, yourself,
and your loved ones. Just as importantly, you don't need to
wait for the huge moments to show gratitude or appreciation.
Be thankful for even the smallest moments or things. Over
time, celebrating or being grateful expands your ability to
accept varying levels of positive energy to stay motivated and
strengthen your commitment. It reinforces your awareness and

appreciation of your current state of being and doing, validates your efforts, fuels your mind and body, and re-energizes you for the next leg of the journey.

While big moments are easy to recognize, I want to share a list of smaller but still important moments that may have slipped under your radar. Be grateful for them. Appreciate them. Celebrate them.

- Waking up at 7 a.m. feeling energized and refreshed.
- Getting your required exercises done before you start work.
- Arriving on time for an appointment.
- When you completed what you set out to do for the day.
- Cooking or eating a delicious meal.
- Having a happy gathering with friends.
- An unexpected message of appreciation from an acquaintance, a colleague, a friend, or a family member.
- A bright sunny day for your outdoor activities.
- Hearing your favourite song on the radio.

In case you have a hard time understanding why the above are worth celebrating, try thinking about how the opposite of those would affect you.

- Waking up feeling lousy, certainly not the best way to start your day.
- Feeling sluggish or guilty of missing your exercises.
- Being late and feeling rushed, not to mention looks of disapproval, depending on the type of appointment.
- More work for the next day.
- Having a bad or tasteless meal; who wants that?
- Leaving a gathering thinking, 'I don't think I want to see those people again.'

- Someone coming to you with a problem or an angry message
- A cloudy or rainy day
- Music changes the mood. You wouldn't want to hear a song you dislike

'The more you praise and celebrate in life, the more there is in life to celebrate.'

—Oprah Winfrey

Reward yourself, but in ways that will not hinder your progress

As mentioned in previous paragraphs, celebrating is important. While there are countless moments to celebrate, there are countless ways to do so. The key is to ensure that your way of celebrating and rewarding yourself reinforces the goals you are trying to achieve.

Pamper yourself with a soothing massage instead of chomping your way through a buffet after a 20 km run if your goal is to stay fit. If you desire to strengthen bonds with your family, plan a travel trip to spend quality time with them after all the late nights at the office instead of buying them gifts. Focus on self-love and sharing the joy of your progress with the people you care about. Their smiles will keep you moving.

Display your 'stars'

When I was a student, my father gave me a gold star sticker for every 'A' I received on my test paper, and I would stick the star on a list and pin the list on the fridge. I loved looking at those stars and was motivated to study harder to get more 'A's and gold stars. Why stop the practice now? Get creative. Instead of displaying your gold stars on a fridge, you can put your accomplishments as a screensaver, print them on a T-shirt, or make an artistic or cute plaque. My friend's husband once won a local cooking contest, and she rewarded him with a personalized apron with the words 'Sandy's best personal chef', which he proudly wears every time he cooks. I've tasted his food several times and they get better and better!

Display your stars. Visualize your achievements. Inspire yourself to pursue the next star.

The glass is half full

Focus on what you have achieved rather than how much you still need to d The glass is either half empty or half full. Why not look at your present situation from a more fulfilled perspective? Fulfilment paves the way to greater momentum.

Maintain momentum with pleasure.

Make the motion magical.

Key takeaways

- Maintaining momentum is as difficult as, if not more so, than starting the action. Finding ways to keep the motor running is critical.
- Starting small to induce motion, practising regularly and correctly, simplifying your thinking, and celebrating occasionally help to sustain morale and motivation.
- Appreciate how far you've come. Maintain a 'glass half full' and fulfilled perspective to continue the momentum.

Chapter N

'No' Is Always an Option

'Freedom isn't the ability to say yes. It's the ability to say no.'
—Anonymous

Everyone wants a piece of you. If you say *yes* all the time, where does that lead you?

One of the most valuable lessons I've learnt in my programme management work is prioritization. When I have a long list of tasks within a tight timeline, I count on my goal-oriented nature and laser focus to complete them.

There are a few tactics I employ.

- Remember the 80/20 rule—I focus on 20 per cent of the tasks that make the most impact or solve 80 per cent of the problems.
- I identify issues that may cause delay and manage risks diligently.
- I arrange the tasks that can be done in parallel.
- I reshuffle priorities and delay other work that is not time-sensitive.
- I call out to my manager or leadership for support on certain projects.

Most important of all, I say *no*, especially to requests that are distractions to my core deliverables. Workwise, they come in all forms, whether speaking at an event, jumping in on non-urgent duties, or organizing after-work activities. These requests derail my momentum for no good reason and don't add value to what I am trying to accomplish.

'But my job is demanding, my boss is demanding, I can't say no to either, and I don't have time for other things at all!'

The above may be true, but . . .

you *always* have a choice.

No doubt, there exists soul-sucking work, bosses who behave like jerks, and jobs that take you away from your personal time or from your family. But, unless you are sold into slavery, you always have a choice. You have a choice to speak with your manager, you have a choice to negotiate with others for a more equitable allocation of work, you have a choice to ask for help, and you have a choice to walk away. The catch is, *when you own your choices, you own your consequences*. Often, you have to make trade-offs. If you choose to say yes to accepting more work due to pressure or because 'that's how it is', then you have made your choice.

Saying 'no' beyond work

Saying 'no' also goes beyond the professional realm. You can say 'no' to your family's demands, you can say 'no' to lending someone money, you can say 'no' to helping someone move their house, heck, you can even say 'no' to a gathering at a time and place that inconveniences you!

You define when you want to say 'no' and *say it*.

Why you say 'yes'

You say 'yes' because you don't wish to offend the other person, you want to foster or maintain your relationship, or you want others to have a favourable opinion of you. You worry that people will stop being nice to you or what they will think of you once you say no to them. In a nutshell, you seek people's approval. You are guilty of being a people pleaser.

You say 'yes' because you don't know how to stand up for yourself or you are caught off-guard. You may be afraid of dealing with angry or unfriendly responses, so you say yes to diffuse any unwanted situation. Without realizing it, you become the person everyone turns to because you are agreeable and perhaps a pushover.

You say 'yes' because of guilt or obligations. You tend to put the needs of others over your own, and hence you find it hard to reject their requests. The guilt feeling is quite common in the case of many parents I know, especially mothers. They feel they need to fulfil their children's requests to be a good parent, so they say yes to them. While being selfless and caring for others is admirable, you risk being depleted if you constantly sacrifice your needs and goals to satisfy the wants of others.

You say 'yes' because you believe you are responsible, or need to be in control of everything. This need for control can happen in almost any job that requires collaboration, especially in group projects. There's almost always a person who wants to make sure that everything is in order or perfect, takes control, takes care of the group, pulls the most weight, and steps in and helps others do their work. They find it hard to say no to meetings at inconvenient hours, to last-minute demands and tasks. This over-active sense of responsibility may turn well-meaning intentions into unnecessary compulsion.

> 'If you say "yes" to everything, you won't get balance. You get off balance.'
> —Jack Welch, ex-CEO of General Electric, and
> Suzy Welch in their book *Winning*

Every time you say 'yes' to requests out of fear, guilt, or doubt, you say 'no' to yourself and what matters to you—your time, relationships, health, and goals. By saying yes, you are allowing the priorities of others to take over your own. You are mired in their wants. You are taking empowerment away from yourself. If you can't cope with all the requests you say yes to, you end up feeling frustrated, stressed, or incompetent. The worrying thing is that all these emotions don't go unnoticed or unfelt. You may try your best to bury them, but their vibes linger on and gather strength. It may take less than you think before your inner volcano erupts.

Saying 'no' is not about being selfish. It's about establishing healthy boundaries, setting expectations, and prioritizing tasks. It's your right to turn down a request, even if it comes from your manager or loved ones. You can do so politely and, if needed, offer them alternatives acceptable to you.

Saying 'no' to things you feel don't matter paves the way to saying 'yes' to the things that matter. Saying no to people liberates you from their wants and empowers you to focus on your wants.

People are drawn to confidence and authenticity.

Saying 'no' for a good reason will not make people dislike you.

Saying 'yes' for no good reason will not make people like you.

How to handle a request and say 'no'

When someone comes to you to ask for something, pause to assess the situation and pause your urge to respond. Assess:

- The validity of the request—What type of request is that? Is it an invitation? Is it important?
- The sincerity and attitude of the person—Is the person in need? What does the person expect?
- Your thoughts—What's going on in my mind right now? How do I feel about this request?

If you are currently tied up, even if the request is valid, the person is sincere, or it's simply your natural response, hold your 'yes'! If you are struggling with this, given below are some tips and pocket phrases for saying 'no'. Remember, you don't have to offer any explanation. Sometimes the more you explain, the worse it gets, especially if you fumble your explanations.

- Just say it. Just say 'no'.
- Thanks for thinking of me, but I have other plans.
- I'm sorry to hear this, but I really can't help you.
- Regrettably, I'm afraid I can't fit this in.
- I have to decline. I don't have the bandwidth for that right now.

If you find it hard to say 'no' immediately, buy yourself some time to think through a response, and then say 'no'.

- Allow me to check my schedule.
- I don't have an answer right now. Let me get back to you.
- I'd like to be more certain before I respond.

Offer alternatives that are acceptable to you. These options may be more suitable if you find it hard to flatly turn down a request from your manager, if the task falls under your remit, or if you are the best and only person who can carry out the task.

- I'm working on something else. If this request is more urgent, I'd like to postpone my current task or hand it over to someone else.
- I can help you, but I'm able to work on your request only next week.
- May I suggest getting John Doe to assist? He has the same skills and knowledge as I do.
- I'm not a big fan of loud bars. May I suggest a café instead?

There will always be people who are pushy, demanding, and very persistent. It takes practice to say 'no' effectively. Be prepared and train yourself to:
- Say 'no' repeatedly.
- Say 'no' confidently.
- Say 'no' politely.

Say NO to say YES to your goals.

Key takeaways

- Learn to say 'no' to requests that don't add value and distract you from your goals.
- You always have a choice in any situation, but owning your choices means owning your consequences.
- Saying 'yes' out of fear, guilt, or doubt means saying 'no' to your other priorities.
- Saying 'no' establishes healthy boundaries, sets expectations, and empowers you to focus on your needs and wants.

Chapter O

Opportunity Favours the Bold and Prepared

'Success occurs when opportunity meets preparation.'
—Zig Ziglar, salesperson, author,
and motivational speaker

'The problem with fairytales isn't that they don't exist. It's that they do exist, but only for some people.'
—Lauren Oliver, young adult novelist,
author of *Panic* and the *Delirium* trilogy

While many of you are familiar with the fairy tale of Cinderella, allow me to take you on a different version for this chapter.

Cinderella's dream was to find and marry Prince Charming. The good news finally arrived when the king and queen held a ball, for their to find a bride. Cinderella believed that her dream would finally come true. Many distinguished men will graced the event, and she was confident to meet her Prince Charming. She even begged her stepmother and stepsisters to let her attend the ball. Although her pleas were refused, Cinderella eventually made it thanks to her fairy godmother.

Arriving at the ball, Cinderella was thrilled! 'This is the opportunity of a lifetime!' she thought. As Cinderella scanned the dance floor, she momentarily locked eyes with . . . Prince Charming! He was immediately captivated by her beauty. To her joy and surprise, he started walking in her direction.

Here comes the opportunity!

Or was it?

Imagine this.

Cinderella was suddenly at a loss. Her heart was racing as the prince walked over. 'Oh no, now what, what do I do?'

The prince came right up in front of her, politely asked for her name, and if she would like to join him for a dance. At that moment, Cinderella's heart was thumping. Thoughts were wrestling inside her head. She didn't know how to dance! She looked at him tenderly, her eyes filled with desire. But when she opened her mouth, she found herself struggling to speak. No words came out!

Embarrassed, Cinderella turned her back to the prince and walked away! She didn't accept his invitation because she had never learnt how to dance. She was too scared and shy! Unfortunately, the prince didn't know that. After being snubbed by Cinderella, he went on to find another lady who was more than prepared and eager to dance with him. Cinderella watched in dismay as her prince danced joyfully with someone else. Since she wasn't dancing with anyone, Cinderella got disheartened and bored. She then decided to leave the ball way before midnight and never left behind one of her glass slippers in haste.

In the end, the prince never danced with Cinderella, never fell in love with her, and never had a reason to trigger his search for her. Cinderella continued her dull life.

Yes, I am perverting a romantic childhood fairy tale to elaborate a point.

Opportunity favours the bold and prepared.

People aren't actively paying attention or setting themselves up for opportunities because they are preoccupied with other matters. Sadly, opportunity doesn't knock on your door, introduce itself, and say 'Grab me!' It doesn't push you towards its path either. It's often in disguise. You have to spot it, and this 'spotting' ability is not innate in all of us. However, the more prepared you are, the more vigilant you get at spotting opportunities. Fortunately, there are ways that one can strengthen this.

(i) Brainstorm the possibilities

Start by writing down your goals. For each one, brainstorm several methods for achieving it and what's required for each method. If going from one to 100 feels like too big a step, break down and look at other interval steps that you can take to move closer. It's essential to include this step as this brainstorming exercise helps you expand your range, encourage creative thoughts, and increase your receptiveness to ideas, options, solutions, and opportunities.

(ii) Be willing to read and research

There are various methods, depending on the time you wish to spend and the type and amount of information required. For a start, there are many articles online or books in the library at your disposal. You can also consider surveys, interviews, and focus groups. Suppose you are thinking about carving a space in the marketplace or offering a varied solution. In that case you need to do your homework on a range of things, for example, competitors, customer profiles, and product categories. Can you upgrade, downgrade, make it mass market, or go after a niche audience?

Let's use toilet paper as an example. When people think about toilet paper, they mostly think about a commoditized and banal product. There's nothing special about it. Yet Renova, a privately-owned Portuguese paper products company, managed to reinvent this category! It 'classed up' white toilet paper into a premium product and produced the world's first black toilet paper Renova Black, which shifted from a novelty item to a luxury fashion item and spun off many other colours. The increased brand equity with Renova Black also boosted sales for other products. That is one opportunity well-spotted and leveraged!

(iii) Reach out

Talk to people. Make contacts. On the one hand, you want to reach out to suitable people. On the other hand, it's a numbers game. The more people you know or the more options you explore, the more opportunities will come your way. One thing leads to another. You'll never know the ideas and possibilities you can generate by casting a wide net. Look at it from a trial-and-error or even as a target practice point of view. Without attempting, you have no opportunity to practice, refine, or assess.

Success is a numbers game

A common complaint I hear from my clients is the lack of success in job searches. My first question to my clients is often—how many applications have you submitted? Of the responses, I don't think I had one mentioning more than fifty. A few of them stopped after barely thirty applications. They were adamant that the odds were against them and were often shocked when I told them that I used to send up to 100 or more applications, even to targeted companies and sectors, to obtain a suitable job with the right remuneration.

The truth is, very few people have odds working for them. It's a numbers game! Let's assume you have sent fifty job applications. If you have decent experience, maybe ten companies got back to you. Out of ten, maybe five companies were not suitable for you or you for them, be it salary, role expectations, or other factors at the initial screening phases. Out of the remaining five companies, you are likely to be subjected to several rounds of interviews and competing against other qualified candidates. Bear in mind that the higher the job level, the harder the process. Finally, the stars aligned! You eventually made it and ended up with one satisfying job offer.

I'm being very optimistic about the above statistics.

Many things in life are a numbers game, be it looking for jobs, investors, customers, or a life partner. Why do you think cold calling still exists? Its average success rate is 2 per cent, which is low. Despite this percentage, cold calling is still a highly effective method to bring in sales. Many businesses firmly embed this form of outbound lead generation into their sales strategy.

Train your guts

Preparation only goes so far. You must be willing to seize the opportunity. You must be bold to take it. Being prepared trains your readiness to seize the opportunity, but being bold *gets you over* to the other side.

"Opportunity knocking? Can you hold?"

CartoonStock.com

Take that leap of faith.

In some situations, people don't grab on to opportunities because they feel that the particular opportunity is not the one they originally sought or that the timing is off. They are hesitant and prefer to wait for the golden opportunity instead of settling for a lesser one. We see this attitude manifesting in many aspects, especially in job hunts. How many people turn down a decent job offer because they are holding out for their dream job? They then regret it later when their dream job never came or realizing that it comes with nightmare consequences.

You just can't know how things will turn out

I remember celebrating with my good friend Winnie when she landed her dream job at a prestigious government ministry in Singapore. She had her sights set on joining the ministry since she started university and was elated when they decided to hire her right after graduation. However, she was completely disillusioned when I met her over dinner three weeks into her role. She told me her colleagues and managers had a dismissive attitude towards her because she wasn't from an Ivy League university, despite her high academic achievement graduating with a First Class Honours. Throughout the two-hour dinner, she also complained about the politics, red tape, and how she dreaded going to work every day. It sucked the soul out of her. She quit after a month. Winnie later became a teacher in a secondary school and had a much more fulfilling career as an educator.

The purpose of this anecdote is not to criticize anyone or any company but to illustrate that what you experience may not always match what you had expected. Conversely, what you didn't expect can end up to be a positive experience! I almost turned down my role at Fuji Xerox due to a horrible interview experience but joining them turned out to be extremely rewarding. I went from editing proposal content to managing the entire proposal process and a huge knowledge management project that eventually won me the Most Valuable Player award. Who knew?

Moral of the story—keep your eyes, heart, and mind open. You may just be amazed.

The truth is, it's rare that the right opportunity knocks at the right time. Therefore, don't stay closed to options. Opportunities of any sort can be a springboard to progress. It's what you make of it and how. If you make sound decisions and take sensible actions, one opportunity gets you another. It may even catapult you to quicker success and wider horizons.

Opportunity rarely presents itself raw.

Stay prepared. Stay bold. Stay open.

Key takeaways

- Opportunities are appear often in disguise. The more prepared you are, the more you can spot them.
- Having clear goals, brainstorming possibilities to reach the goals, researching, networking, and persisting expand your range and increase your receptiveness to ideas, solutions, and opportunities.
- Being prepared is one side of the equation; being bold to seize the opportunity completes the equation.
- Having a 'golden' opportunity is rare. Stay open to options. One opportunity gets you to another if you make sensible decisions and take solid action.

Chapter P

Plan for the Best, Prepare for the Worst

'Shoulda, coulda, woulda.'
—a common and perhaps sarcastic expression
to dismiss one's worries or regrets

To reach your goals, you need tenacity, a positive mindset, and discipline, among many other things. You also need to consider roadblocks and what can derail your plan. Have a solid strategy to handle the potential obstacles in your way. In a nutshell, you need to plan well, but be prepared for various eventualities, especially the worst.

It's not about being a doomsday prepper. It's about being realistic. With any goal we go after, there's a chance that we will face obstacles; even the most optimistic person has an ounce of doubt. It's naïve to think that our voyage from start to end will be smooth sailing.

Just think about it, if Titanic's operators were prepared for the worst and carried more lifeboats, there would be many more survivors.

What if, what if, what if?

Hindsight is always 20/20. We can debate that there is an opportunity cost to every option. However, preparation is better than cure. It permits us to function from a foundation of security. We can channel more energy to focus on the positive items knowing that we have planned for the 'what ifs' and lessened the unease. No doubt, there are unprecedented crises whose reach, damage, and duration are beyond anyone's prediction, such as the COVID-19 pandemic. But crises are not an excuse to lament that things are out of our control and leave them to fate. In fact, we should remind ourselves to be more responsive.

Train your mind to see the good in every situation

When disaster strikes, you are allowed to feel angry, depressed, or lost. It takes time to come to terms with it. However, wallowing in long-term self-pity is one of the most futile things you can do for yourself. You can't change what you can't change; the only thing you can change is your mindset. Train your mind to see the good in every situation no matter how hard it is. If you were to ask, 'What's the good in this?' or 'What's there to appreciate about this?' you would approach every situation with a pair of lenses that focus your attention on the positives. As the law of attraction implies, if you focus your energy on the good, the good will come to you. Seek and you will find.

Every cloud has a silver lining, even for hazards as destructive as the COVID-19 pandemic. Lives were gone, plans were destroyed, and jobs were lost. Yet, many positive things came out of it.

- **A flexible work structure.**
  Before the COVID-19 pandemic, the idea of working from home was unacceptable. Right now, more and more employees expect this type of arrangement. Some companies documented this flexibility in the contracts to allow employees to work from home a certain number of days a week. Some companies are even fine with employees telecommuting full-time. This new type of flexibility is wonderful news for people who live far away from the office. The flexibility has also opened more job opportunities to people living in the suburbs or other cities.
- **Innovations in online conferencing, communications, and collaboration tools as physical meetings reduce.**
  Technological improvements in these tools will lead to higher definition videos, enhanced video and sound

quality of live events streaming, more palpable virtual and augmented reality experiences, increased precision in automatic speech recognition and computer vision, and faster and smoother workflows.

- **More time for self-reflection.**
The pandemic has pushed many people to reflect and re-evaluate many aspects of their lives. It forces us to re-think our values, purpose, and definition of happiness. It gives us clarity on what's most important. Viewing the pandemic through the lens of a silver lining allowed us to redefine our lives, reconnect with loved ones, and pursue success and happiness on our terms.

- **Heightened awareness of the plight of 'essential workers' and appreciation for the crucial role they play in society.**
Many of these workers, traditionally not in highly regarded or well-paid jobs, kept the engines of society working. Any form of recognition is well-deserved and the call for their increased financial compensation, along with mental and emotional support, could not have been more apt.

If you believe that everything happens for a reason, when faced with an unfortunate situation, tell yourself to look for the best thing that can come out of this—it can be a new opportunity for you, an awakening process, and perhaps touching stories and lessons for you to share with your children and grandchildren.

There must be something better in store for me

I have a friend Oliver who is a freelance sales trainer. Oliver was ecstatic to have clinched a big training contract with a multinational corporation. However, three months before he was scheduled to train at their premises, Coronavirus, the name at the time, started to surge. The multinational corporation cancelled his contract, and he began to lose his other training gigs as fear poured and restrictions tightened. As Oliver looked at his eroding businesses for the year, his heart sank like the Titanic.

It was a very trying period in 2020. No one knew what the next month or week would look like. Situations were erratic, and many were people impacted palpably by the Coronavirus were on edge.

Life sometimes deals you a rough hand. Nothing is guaranteed, and everything is uncertain. But during these times, we have to pause, stay calm, and brainstorm ways to usher ourselves to a more favourable situation.

(i) Identify what's within your control and act.

Continuing with the example of Oliver, he knew that he had to be more proactive about the situation. After three to four months of finding his way in the dark and waiting to see what happens next, he started exploring what he could.

Oliver redesigned his training courses to suit the online pedagogy and diversified his courses. With no physical constraints and no need to travel, he could offer a better deal to the companies by increasing the number of participants per session and the number of sessions. Since he is bilingual, he started to craft training courses in Mandarin and reached out to Chinese companies.

(ii) Influence what you can't control.

Although Oliver could not control the decision of the companies to hire him, he worked on his pitch to make his offering as attractive as possible. He also polished his customer service skills and was attentive to the requests of his clients. Even when potential companies or clients rejected him, he politely asked for feedback and refined his courses or approaches. Wherever possible, he ensured he left a positive impression. Furthermore, he redesigned his website, increased his social media presence, and joined several online clubs and events to expand his network and attract people to his training courses.

(iii) If steps one and two don't go your way, think of your alternative or the next best outcome to minimize the negative impact.

Fortunately for Oliver, ever since he became a freelancer, he has always made it a point to accumulate sufficient savings and liquid assets for unexpected emergencies. However, no one in 2020 could confidently predict how long the pandemic would last. Hence, Oliver tightened his belt and rented out his spare room to compensate for his near-zero revenue for nearly eight months. It helped him cushion this period. Things gradually picked up towards the end of 2020. By mid-2022, his revenue increased by about 30 per cent compared to the pre-pandemic period, thanks to his diversified offerings and wider audience.

Oliver emerged from the depth of the pandemic not just relatively unscathed but ended up with more blessings because of his preparedness and responsiveness.

> 'Remember, when disaster strikes, the time to prepare has passed.'
> —a popular quote attributed to Steven Cyros, businessperson

If you have a plan-for-the-best-prepare-for-the-worst approach while setting your goals, it moves you quicker from a paralysis mode to a proactive mode when a shocking incident strikes. You are likely to react promptly, activate necessary plans, and take well-calculated actions to minimize the probability of an unfortunate incident snowballing into an unmanageable crisis.

Key takeaways

- Reaching your goals requires tenacity, a positive mindset, discipline, a firm plan, and a strategy to handle potential obstacles.
- Preparation permits us to function from a foundation of security, allowing us to focus on the goals.
- Although we can't control Black Swan events like the COVID-19 pandemic, we should always remind and train ourselves to be prepared and responsive.
- Should disasters strike, identify what's within your control and act, influence what you can't control, and think of the next best options to minimize its negative impact.
- Being prepared moves you quicker from a paralysis mode to a proactive mode when disasters strike.

Chapter Q

Quality versus Quantity, You Decide

'Quality takes time and reduces quantity, so it makes you, in a sense, less efficient. The efficiency-optimized organization recognizes quality as its enemy.'
—Tom DeMarco, management consultant
to many Fortune 500 companies

'Quality is everyone's responsibility.'
—W. Edwards Deming, one of the founding fathers
of Total Quality Management

Quality or quantity? You will likely experience this dilemma at various points on the way to your goals.

There is discourse out there that seems to favour quality over quantity. You save space by possessing a few pieces of durable items than many flimsy ones. You save energy and time by choosing to hang out with a tight group of reliable friends than a big bunch of fair-weather acquaintances. You probably make more money selling to your top ten customers than a string of long-tail customers. Preferring quality over quantity is also more sustainable for the planet. People should declutter and embrace a more minimalist lifestyle. You avoid overwhelming yourself and have less stress. Hence, going for quality makes sense.

While I agree with the above examples, the truth is it really depends. While quality is important, there are some situations where quantity takes precedence.

What's the argument that favours quantity?

Quality is subjective across many contexts

If you are a columnist, you can spend a week writing and editing an article to make it of 'quality', but your readers may not share the same opinion. Quality is in the eye of the beholder. Spending more time to perfect an article does not guarantee appreciation for your extra efforts. If you were paid per article, you would have been better off providing regular content for your readers.

Depending on the type of business, we can apply the same logic. News websites rely on regular stories to keep them in business. A bigger database of news stories provides more content for readers to engage, keeping them longer on your website. There is no guarantee that focused coverage on the war in country X beats an article about organic furniture on readership.

Every additional piece of content is an opportunity. While there has to be a minimum balance between quantity and quality, excessive quality control that reduces content throughput can be counterproductive. In short, don't simply sacrifice quantity for quality.

The need for speed

Speed is key in today's business, especially regarding product innovation. If you take years to conceptualize, build, and perfect a product before taking it to market, your competitors may have done so several times, gotten valuable feedback, and revised their product to better suit the end-users. While you are deliberating the first ideal version, they are building, learning, refining, and building more advanced versions. Again, what you think is of 'quality' to go to market is subjective. Sometimes, consumers may prefer a stream of products with incremental quality over waiting for that one product of supposedly top quality.

Quantity matters in the digital age

People have increasingly short attention spans. The popularity of TikTok, a social media app which allows you to watch, create, and share videos, points to a growing number of people who crave short bursts of entertainment. A large quantity of videos is key for people who scroll through them incessantly.

The algorithms in social media apps are complex, with various factors influencing how content is served to users. Whether the videos are of a certain quality is irrelevant and impossible to be decided by one person; it's up to millions of users to judge, and to each his own. All that matters is new and more content.

Quality can be limiting in its reach and scale

As mentioned in Chapter O, success is a numbers game. Sometimes you need big volumes to generate opportunities, leads, or other indicators you are measuring. We see the quantity approach used often in the case of content marketing. High and frequent content drives traffic, increases brand awareness and visibility, and boosts audience engagement. I don't deny that quality is important, but before you can get to quality, you will need the quantity to support that.

Going for quantity is especially true for programmes and policies that target the masses. You are judged on quantity fulfilled, not quality matched. It is more logical to provide 500 people with basic meals than fifty people with quality meals if you are trying to feed the less fortunate. Similarly, suppose you are trying to address high unemployment. In this case, you will prioritize placing as many people as possible into largely suitable jobs. Ticking all the boxes for job seekers and employers is a separate concern.

Quality is the language of the affluent

Quality can be expensive. Those who speak of wanting quality are typically those who can afford it. For the money-sensitive folks, would you spend $20 on 1 kg of organic vegetables or a mix of non-organic vegetables, fruits, and meat?

Let's switch items and look at clothing. Why is fast fashion so appealing? It has grown exponentially over the past twenty years, with brands such as Zara, UNIQLO, and H&M dominating the markets. Compared to brands like Ralph Lauren, Prada, and Chanel, clothes from fast fashion brands don't have the same quality. But, mass shoppers don't care and don't expect them to! The appeal of fast fashion lies in it being inexpensive, has a wide variety of designs according to the latest trends, and can be changed or disposed of without giving much thought. The churn rate within the wardrobes is high. Because these clothes are affordable, shoppers can purchase new outfits easily and update their style any time. Quality, amongst many other things like design or comfort, is subjective. Who's to say that wearing fast fashion brands makes you less trendy?

Despite all the reasons, I'm not asking you to prioritize quantity over quality. I'm just trying to present quantity in a fair light.

Don't disregard quality, but don't dismiss quantity.

There is no preferred choice for all cases. Choosing quantity or quality depends on the context and your goals. Sometimes, you choose both.

You decide.

Key takeaways

- Quality may be important, but quantity takes precedence in some situations.
- Arguments that favour quantity include the need for speed, scale, and variety. Quality is subjective across many contexts and often comes with higher costs, making it hard to justify prioritizing or choosing quality.
- There is no preferred choice. Choosing quantity or quality or both depends on the context and your goals.

Chapter R
Rest, Recharge, and Review

'Take rest; a field that has rested gives a bountiful crop.'
—Ovid, ancient Roman poet

I've always liked the fable 'The Tortoise and the Hare' by famous Greek storyteller Aesop. The fable revolves around a race between the two animals. The tortoise was tired of constantly being made fun of by the hare for its slow speed. It decided to challenge the hare to a race. Positive that it would win, the hare agreed readily to the challenge.

On race day, as soon as it began, the hare ran very fast and was way ahead of the tortoise. Confident that the tortoise would take a long time to come near it, the hare decided to take a nap. During this time, the tortoise kept going slowly and steadily. When the hare finally woke up, it realized the tortoise had long moved past it and just crossed the finish line.

This simple fable highlighted worthy lessons. It taught me not to be complacent, it taught me that slow and steady can win the race, and it taught me perseverance and hard work. If I have to infer another lesson from the fable, it will be to know *when* to rest.

Even machines need to rest

Many science fiction movies I watched painted a dystopian scenario where machines take over the world. It gave me the impression that they are omnipotent because they don't eat, sleep, or fall sick.

Hence, I was surprised to find out that the typical utilization rate for printers, based on industry-standard calculation, for a large office environment for 500 staff and above is 3–7 per cent! If you are wondering how I got the percentage, I used to work on managed print services deals.

Based on a couple of blogs I read on machine utilization, the average utilization rate is 26–28 per cent. If I think of how long I'm on my laptop (weekends included), the percentage is not too far off, although I suspect the laptop utilization rate is much higher. Machines running at 100 per cent or even just 80 per cent are more prone to breakdown, wear and tear, or slower processing. Ultimately, what's considered optimal utilization depends on the type of machine. The main point I'm trying to make is that even machines need to rest, let alone humans! If we assume that humans work eight hours a day, our average utilization rate of 33 per cent still beats that of the machines!

The next time you're tempted to tell someone, 'You should rest. You're not a machine', think again.

We're probably working harder.

We should say, 'You should rest. You're already working harder than the average machine.'

Planned rest is vital

Objectively speaking, it was not wrong for the hare to take a break, especially if it has been running. Here's the crucial part. It should have chosen the right moment to rest, probably after the finish line! Resting is a tactic and should be done strategically.

No matter what you try to achieve, you need to rest at suitable points. It's impossible to perform continuously at full capacity without the law of diminishing returns setting in after some time.

Law of diminishing returns

The law of diminishing returns is an economic principle that states that after an optimal level of capacity is reached, any additional input will result in smaller increases in output.

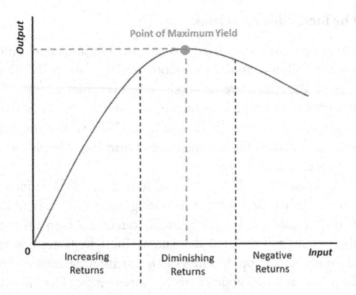

Illustrating the law of diminishing returns

For example, you are able to read fifty pages of a book per hour for four hours. After four hours, you can read only forty-five pages per hour and gradually fewer pages as the hours go by. The reduced number of pages means your optimal level of capacity is reached by the end of the fourth hour. Assuming all other variables are constant, your input, that is, time spent reading, after four hours yields smaller increases in output, that is, pages read. The law of diminishing returns has set in. If you continue to read without pausing, you become less efficient by the hour and potentially subject yourself to other undesirable consequences.

Doing more is not always better if it impacts your productivity, longevity, and even well-being in the long run. Having sufficient downtime is part of a long-term growth plan. You need to wind down and rest well to recharge and restore balance. Pausing allows you to take this time for self-care, review your plans, and re-strategize to set yourself up for peak performance.

The incredible comeback

After a series of losses, Roger Federer, one of the greatest tennis players of all time, took a six-month break in the second half of 2016 to allow his knee and body to recover from injuries that he sustained. Rest and restoration as a strategy work! No one expected him to come back roaring in 2017 with immediate success. Federer lifted the Australian Open and Wimbledon in January and July that year.

LeBron James, NBA star and four-time MVP winner, is known for his commitment to resting and recovery, resulting in the success and longevity of his career. To keep up with his rigorous training and demanding lifestyle, James ensures he winds down appropriately with nutrition, relaxation, and sleep. In a 2018 podcast with entrepreneur Tim Ferriss, James revealed that he aimed to get eight to ten hours of good quality sleep a night, and he isn't an oddball. Athletes from various sports, including Federer, sprinter Usain Bolt, and swimmer Michael Phelps, regularly get at least eight to ten hours of sleep every night, excluding naps.

Sleep is a fantastic problem solver

In his speech at a Hong Kong Young Entrepreneurs event, Alibaba founder Jack Ma spoke about how he persevered through the years with the e-commerce company despite wanting to give up countless times. Ma revealed that whenever he encountered a major problem or difficulty, he would go to sleep and then think about the problem in the morning. One's brain needs a break from all the clutter, noise, and people. Sleep helped Ma to recharge and face his problems with renewed energy and perspective.

The key to persevering in your goals can be that simple and straightforward.

Take your break.

There are valuable habits we can extract from athletes and businesspeople, and they don't cost a fortune. Most of us have the means to allow ourselves proper rest, recovery, and recharge. Sleep, nutrition, meditation, and exercise are some examples of readily available and manageable activities that can make a difference to our overall well-being and increase our resilience to burnout and breakdowns.

Tips to top up your tank

1. Get sufficient sleep. You may not need as many hours as the athletes constantly pushing their bodies, but most adults from ages eighteen to sixty-five need seven to nine hours of sleep a night.
2. Develop a healthy diet. Good nutrition impacts your mood and energy level throughout the day.
3. Get active. Exercise, stretch, or anything to boost oxygen circulation and increase the energy flow.
4. Step away from your phones and laptops. Connect with the wider surroundings and engage with people instead of looking and typing on small screens.
5. Meditate and practise mindfulness to help you regulate emotions and cope with stress.
6. Take a walk in nature. Vitamin D, fresh air, and soothing greenery reduce tension and enhance the immune system.
7. Take a break from whatever is draining you, be a situation or a person. Use that break to take your mind off until you regain the energy.
8. Maintain a journal. It's a good way to express your feelings. The action of writing helps to process your emotions and problems.

9. Take a warm bath. You can enhance the ambience by lighting scented candles to soothe your mood.
10. Have fun! Do the things that bring you joy and comfort. It can be a massage, an outing with friends, a holiday, or a movie you want to watch.
11. It's okay to do absolutely nothing.
12. Don't stop at this list.

Resilience is not about how long you can slog it out until you reach your goals; it's about incorporating intervals to ensure you are properly re-energized before continuing. Rest is critical for one's healing and restoration to spur further growth.

Before you hurry on to your next task, pause. Use this time to rest, recharge, and reflect on the journey. Think about what went well, what can be handled better, and the types of emotions you faced. Strategize the next leg of your journey wisely.

'Taking time to do nothing often brings everything into perspective.'
—Doe Zantamata, author, photographer, and graphic designer

Rest to do your best.

Key takeaways

- Planned rest and sufficient downtime are vital to perform optimally and prevent burnout.
- Resting and restoration are effective strategies that can lead to incredible comebacks and longevity in career, as shown by athletes like Roger Federer and LeBron James.

- The options to rest and recharge are accessible to many people. Simple and readily available activities such as sleep, nutrition, exercise, meditation, and spending time in nature can make significantly impact overall well-being and increase resilience to burnout.

Chapter S
Sharpen Your Axe

'Give me six hours to chop down a tree and I will spend the first four sharpening the axe.'
—Abraham Lincoln, 16th President of the United States

The pizza maker

There was a chef who was well-known for his pizzas. He had been running the business for a few years, had a steady stream of customers, and could sell up to 500 pizzas every day.

However, as the years went on, his sale of pizzas gradually decreased. It went from 500 a day to 450, then 400, 350 ...

These days, he is lucky if he can sell 200 pizzas a day.

'It doesn't make sense', the chef said to his wife, 'I kept the same recipe, used the same ingredients, and maintained the cost. I don't understand why my business is getting poorer.'

His wife pondered and asked, 'When was the last time you explored and tasted pizzas besides your own?'

'Explore? I had no time to do so. I've been busy making and selling my own pizzas.'

This story is a reminder to constantly sharpen your axe—your axe being your skills, your knowledge, or you in general. You need to ensure you stay sharp, well, and healthy to perform optimally for the short and long term. *Maintenance is critical.*

Laws are meant to be broken

In the previous chapter, I spoke about the law of diminishing returns occurring after some time. However, there is a way to counter this law or minimize its impact and that is to enhance the input—*you*. By improving the input, productivity and output can remain consistent for a longer time or be raised.

In the chef's example, improving the inputs can mean improving his pizza-making techniques, innovating new recipes, exploring and tasting other pizzas, and learning from successful pizza makers. In our cases, we can sharpen our axes through various activities. The seventh habit, 'Sharpen your saw' in Stephen Covey's book *The 7 Habits of Highly Effective People*, highlighted the importance of enhancing and renewing ourselves through four dimensions—physical, spiritual, mental, and social to allow our capacity to grow and be more effective in dealing with the various demands of our daily lives. I have suggested some activities related to each dimension.

Physical	• Sleep sufficiently • Exercise regularly • Quit smoking • Limit alcohol intake
Spiritual	• Be with nature • Listen to music • Meditate • Pray
Mental	• Read books • Take part in competitions • Enrol in courses, pick up skills such as public speaking, foreign language, project management, basic coding • Engage in games that work your brain such as chess, Sudoku, and Scrabble
Social/Emotional	• Ask for feedback at work or when doing something new • Cultivate strong relationships • Expand your network and make new friends • Contribute to your community

As we engage in axe-sharpening activities, we must also remember a critical component—constant revision and practice—in whatever we do, lest any blunt spots hinder our advancement.

Practice makes progress. You discover and learn more each time by doing, cementing your knowledge, and improving your mastery. Over time and with the right practice and guidance, you develop the memory muscle needed to perform tasks with minimal effort.

Forget me not

It's exceptional to find people blessed with impressive memory to the extent that they can remember past events in detail on what they saw and how they did something. Most of us forget after some time, particularly when trying to learn a new skill or absorb new knowledge.

German psychologist Hermann Ebbinghaus wanted to understand why we forget things and how to prevent them. His research produced the forgetting curve: a graph that shows the decrease in the ability of the brain to retain information

Illustrating Ebbinghaus Forgetting Curve—How much do we retain?

over time. It can happen in days or weeks unless the learnt knowledge is consciously reviewed repeatedly. The curve shows that more than 50 per cent of what we learn is forgotten within an hour, 67 per cent by the end of the day, and 80 per cent by the end of the month.

Forgetting is natural, but fret not; from Ebbinghaus' discovery, there are methods to strengthen your memory and hone your skills.

(i) Spaced learning

Ah, the memories of school days. Homework and tests come to mind! In the past, whenever my teachers taught the class something new, they would give us homework to complete and hand in within twenty-four to forty-eight hours. The daily homework is in addition to homework for the weekend, tests once a month, a mid-term every six months, and of course, the big annual exam! In hindsight, despite the stress, it was a good way to enforce spaced learning.

Calibrate the above approach to suit your learning needs. Our memory fades quickly, but a review session soon after the original learning can improve it. Revising what you have learnt at spaced intervals can reduce the rate at which you forget.

(ii) Overlearn

Put in twice the effort on learning and practising at the beginning. Overlearning can apply to everything from a new language to a new technical concept or Krav Maga techniques. Give extra attention to digesting difficult information and practise multiple times for complex tasks. Instead of memorizing the information or the steps, understand the reasoning and connection: why is it done, solved, or expressed this way? Understanding and processing the mechanics behind something new facilitate memory retention, thus building the required muscle memory.

(iii) Connect the information

There are many ways to do this. You can structure and organize your learnings and thoughts by grouping the related concepts like mind mapping. You can utilize mnemonic devices such as images, acronyms, and rhymes, and the list goes on.

(iv) Take care of yourself

Activities to sharpen your axes, such as sleep, nutrition, and exercise, are critical to boosting memory and learning. You may refer to the activities listed in the physical, spiritual, mental, and social dimensions earlier in the chapter or 'Tips to top up your tank' in Chapter R for more examples.

Perfection doesn't exist, but continuous improvement does

Remember the Kaizen philosophy of continuous improvement mentioned in Chapter I? Never stop learning. There is always room to develop, especially in a fast-evolving world, even when you reach proficiency. You read, network, seek feedback from peers, attend seminars and training courses, do whatever you can to ensure you stay abreast of the changes and leverage the new tools, knowledge, and connections to help you be successful in your quests. Sharpening your axe is a sure way to prevent yourself from stagnating and deteriorating. Don't let what you learn and master fade away.

> 'Formal education will make you a living; self-education will make you a fortune.'
> —Jim Rohn entrepreneur, author, and motivational speaker

You are your best asset. Sharpen your skills.

Key takeaways

- We must constantly sharpen our skills, knowledge, and overall well-being to remain or become more productive over time.
- Renewing ourselves in physical, spiritual, mental, and social areas enhances our ability to deal with the various demands of our daily lives.
- Constant revision and practice improve mastery, develop the memory muscle, and cement knowledge.
- Forgetting things happen to everyone, but methods such as spaced learning and overlearning can help to strengthen memory and hone skills.

Chapter T
Trust Your Instincts

'Intuitions are not to be ignored John. They represent data processed too fast for the conscious mind to comprehend.'
—Sherlock Holmes, famous fictional detective created by author Sir Author Conan Doyle

To say that data and information are necessities is an understatement. The world depends on data like how my late grandmother depended on her eyeglasses. Things seemed fuzzy and didn't make sense without it.

There is no denying data. Without data, there is no information. Without information, there is no insight. One can't analyse, track, plan, validate, decide, and so on. We may still be able to survive today, but we sure can't live a life. As for our goals, we may have to be creative in how we proceed and track if we cannot rely on data to guide us.

Welcome to the matrix

I wasn't born into this 'virtual' world. I'm a digital immigrant. I started using computers at age thirteen. Yet, I'm amazed at how far we have come and what we have created: how technology helps businesses and society advance; and how data and artificial intelligence automates many tasks. All the combined data, information, and technology produce insights that we can leverage to perform and live better.

It's convenient to rely on facts and figures, especially if they help direct us to what we want to achieve in a data-ubiquitous and data-driven world. Having spent a considerable time of my career in the technology sector where big data dominates, I worked closely with people whose work revolved around using data to train machines, predict user behaviour, and make business decisions, among many others.

There is an obsession with wanting to quantify everything, from return on investment for projects to hiring to employee wellness. There's a good reason for it. Having the right datasets and looking at the right data points can assist one with making objective decisions. No one around me was bold or dense enough to declare making a decision based on intuition or what some people commonly refer to as 'gut feel'.

Yet, in a world of big data and the Internet of Things, instinct-driven decisions happen more often than you think.

> 'You know something. What you know, you can't explain, but you feel it.'
> —Morpheus, a character from the *Matrix* franchise

Don't ignore those feelings

Have you ever felt that despite all the data, there are sensations in your body that tell you otherwise? It can be choosing to hire Jane over John despite his impressive interview skills or stopping an activity because you feel something is amiss. Your body is giving you clues, don't ignore them. The answer to those clues may not be apparent immediately, but you must examine that emotion and understand what triggered it.

A huge part of human behaviour is powered by the subconscious mind, which affects many areas, such as memory, decision-making, and creativity. You perceive the world using your five senses, but there's only so much your conscious mind can absorb. The rest resides in your subconscious. That is where your instincts come in. Your instincts guide you when your conscious mind can't process all the information simultaneously.

There's a neurological basis for intuition. Over 100 million neurons in the gut are connected to the brain and transmit signals. Some medical experts term our gut as the 'second brain'. Your gut works with your brain to scour your stored reservoir of experiences, memories, and knowledge while simultaneously processing and comparing incoming information to arrive at an answer. Much unseen work has transpired in the brain. From this angle, intuition or 'gut feel' can be seen as an alternate form of emotional and experiential data that makes trusting it acceptable.

Data is not unbiased

While data are often perceived as independent and impartial, they are the products of complex social processes and decisions, such as how they are collected, treated, analysed, and visualized, reflecting the beliefs, assumptions, or actions of people who produce and manage them.

Data can mislead people depending on how they are used, for example, in the case of statistics, which results from data interpretation and presentation.

You probably have heard this popular quote by Aaron Levenstein, author and professor at Baruch University, 'Statistics are like a bikini. What they reveal is suggestive, but what they conceal is vital.'

To an undiscerning audience, it's easy to manipulate data to serve various interests. More astute individuals who deliberate on data-driven conclusions need time to research, deep dive, and dissect the data from many slants to have a more accurate and impartial picture. While we want a full picture, practicalities dictate that we can't over-analyse and stall crucial actions. It's a trade-off between effort and certainty.

Don't get me wrong. Data and other tangible facts still have to matter

Instincts are not foolproof. The mind is an imperfect processor. It can be fickle, biased, influenced by past or recent events and experiences and it distorts how we process issues and situations. So yes, data definitely matter. Moreover, there are numerous functions and roles that rely on data rather than instincts to operate. There are powerful tools to assist analysts, scientists, and executives in sieving through vast amounts of data to make rational choices amid complexity. If we possess the technology and models to analyse more data in less time to make certain types of decisions, we should make full use of them.

You will be taking loads of actions and making plenty of decisions en route to your goals. Remember, you should never disregard data, just as you should never dismiss your instincts.

There is no 'right' moment to use your instincts

Instincts are hardwired into us by evolution and are always there, albeit in the background. It's a matter of where, when, and how they show up versus how we interpret their significance at that time of being hit by them. There is no right time, but there are some instances when you may wish to pay attention to your instincts and decide how you want to act on them.

(i)   When there is a lack of or no data:
   • She blanks out for no reason.
   • The mood seems to have shifted.
   • Something seems staged about this.
   • That sinking feeling in your stomach.
(ii) When something triggers your conscience:
   • I could, but I shouldn't.
   • This doesn't seem appropriate.
   • Why do I feel bad about this?
   • Doing this makes no sense.
(iii) Life and death situations:
   • A child is drowning.
   • The car brakes are not working.

- There's a huge explosion nearby.
- You heard gunshots.
- There's a big black bear 100 metres in front of you.

(iv) That familiar feeling of knowing, especially when you've done your homework:

- This person is trustworthy.
- I've made the right decision.
- Something is amiss; this will not work.
- What he mentioned sounds neither sincere nor real.

(v) When you feel something is off in your body:

- A constant pain, even if it's a dull one.
- Episodes of lack of breath, and dizziness.
- Certain sensations caused by stress, danger, or other triggers.

'How come when you're right it's female intuition and when I'm right it's dumb luck?'

Leverage your instincts

Marrying instinct and logic can be as successful a pairing as salt and pepper. Sometimes, you need both to support you in making quicker, faster, and more reliable decisions when you feel something is amiss or there is no clear option. If you are still concerned about the amorphous nature of instinct, I came across a few ways in a *Harvard Business Review* article by Melody Wilding, titled 'How to Stop Overthinking and Start Trusting Your Gut', to develop this sense.

(i) Tap into your instincts to make smaller decisions

Many of us rarely have big decisions to make. By using our instincts for frequent and smaller decisions, we train our instincts to be more sensitive before making our way to weightier and more stressful decisions.

(ii) Differentiate between instinct and fear

There are times when we have a battle inside our heads. A part of you wants to go in one direction, and the other part keeps pulling back. Learning to tell instinct from fear gives you more inner clarity. Instinct speaks to you in a different tone. There is more certainty and calmness, and you feel grounded. On the other hand, fear makes you feel anxious and threatened, instilling negative thoughts of what can go wrong.

(iii) Connect instincts with values

Sometimes you are unable to tell why something triggered a reaction. A possibility is that one or more of your values have been touched, positively or negatively. Let's assume you have an uneasy feeling about a team. You find your teammates to be distant. It could mean that one of your core values is connection, which is not apparent in the team. Through an awareness of your values, you have a richer understanding of your thoughts and emotions.

'There's a voice that doesn't use words. Listen.'
—Rumi, Persian poet

Instinct is your *sixth* sense. Trust it. Work with it.

Key takeaways

- Data is ubiquitous and almost indispensable in today's world. People rely on data to analyse, track, predict, decide, and act on countless matters.
- In a data-driven world, instinct-driven decisions remain prevalent.
- With over 100 million neurons in the gut connected to the brain, transmitting signals and processing information, 'gut' feelings or intuitions can be considered an alternate form of emotional and experiential data.
- Although data is not necessarily impartial and can be manipulated, instincts are not foolproof either. We should never dismiss instincts, just as we should never disregard data.
- There is no right moment to use one's instincts. It's up to us to decide how we wish to act upon instincts when they show up.

Chapter U

Untie Your Knots and Unleash Your Potential

'A summit is so much more than a view. I may be biased, but when people say they summit mountains for the view, I don't believe them. No one suffers the way one does on a mountain simply for a beautiful view. A summit isn't just a place on a mountain. A summit exists in our hearts and minds. It is a tiny scrap of a dream made real, indisputable proof that our lives have meaning. A summit is a symbol that with the force of our will and the power of our legs, our backs, and our two hands, we can transform our lives into whatever we choose them to be, whatever our hands are strong enough to create.'

—Erik Weihenmayer, the first blind person to
reach the summit of Mount Everest,
on 25 May 2001

I remember vividly the time when I was hiking on Maria Island in Tasmania, an island state 240 km south of Australia. Maria Island is a natural wildlife sanctuary with bountiful flora and fauna, historic ruins, sweeping bays, and remarkable cliffs. Among the hiking options on the island, I decided to embark on the Bishop and Clerk trail, an 11 km trek that will take me to the summit of the towering dolerite columns on the northern coast, an elevation of about 630 metres or 2,100 feet.

Keen to see the view, I began the relentless incline. I passed through open grasslands and dense forest, and although it was uphill for a big part, it wasn't overly steep. The adrenalin kept me going. I could imagine my exhilaration when I finally ascended. As I reached my final resting point, I scanned the terrain.

Well, trouble.

The last stretch was steep and strewn with broken rocks and boulders. There was no avoiding this path; the way up was completely covered with rubble! It was difficult to navigate the terrain. I decided to try, but the path got loose after I hiked for about 100 metres, and I could feel the rocks sliding from my feet.

I had one thought on my mind—*was it worth it?* I had walked around the island for over half a day before attempting this trek, and I was tired. I paused for ten minutes to enjoy the view and deliberate if I should continue to the top. I had already come so far, seen some great views, and I was satisfied. Why should I spend another thirty minutes climbing and risking the steep and rocky terrain?

I decided to descend. Wanting a final glance, I turned back and looked up wistfully. The views at the top of the summit must look so majestic compared to my current spot! Many thoughts ran through my mind.

Was I too tired? Yes, but not depleted.

Was I scared of the terrain? Hmm . . . not really.

What's holding me back? I can be satisfied with less.

I can be satisfied with less.

That is a self-limiting belief. It tells me that I don't have to go all the way.

I told myself that I could be satisfied with less because I wasn't sure if I had the grit to reach the top, and I wanted to avoid disappointment if I failed.

For a moment, I stood still.

The Great Mental Wall

Self-limiting beliefs are negative self-perceptions that reside in our conscious and subconscious. Many of us are victims of this belief due to unpleasant experiences, hurtful comments, or even values and beliefs inherited from our family and friends. Whether or not the trigger came from school, family, work, or relationships, something impacted us while we were growing up. Perhaps you saw your parents fight over money, perhaps you were made fun of at school because you weren't good-looking or smart, or perhaps your partner told you the relationship was over.

Remember these annoying voices?

'Stop! It's dangerous!'
'Who told you that you can do that?'
'Don't be stupid! Why do you want to go for that?'
'Stop crying! You deserve it.'
'We can't afford this. Stop dreaming.'
'You really think everything is in your control?'
'This is never going to work out.'

These annoying voices, which eventually turned into our inner voices, form the foundation of our mental wall. Because of the wall, we stop ourselves from advancing and giving our best shot. Our actions and decisions are not driven by motivation or ambitions; they are driven by fear. Because of fear, we develop certain beliefs to shield us from further pain or disappointment, and we compensate by telling ourselves it's no big deal and we can live with whatever we choose.

'It's okay that I'm not promoted. I don't wish to work twice as hard.'
'I didn't go to an Ivy League school. I can't expect to find jobs at a top firm.'
'I'm too old to be pursuing a degree in Economics. That ship has sailed.'

'I'm plain looking and I'm shy. If I leave him, I doubt I'll ever find someone who will be attracted to me.'

'I don't wish just to be a housewife, but I don't think I can juggle being a mother and a job.'

'I don't have enough savings, how can I set up my own business?'

If you think you can't, you're probably right

Nine out of ten people will tell you that you can't because *mediocrity is the norm.* Excellence takes work, but beyond that, it takes a mindset. Don't be limited by what's in your mind. Allow me to illustrate this using a story.

The fish in the tank

A child watches as his mother sets up a big fish tank. First, she places the aquarium gravel, plant ornaments, and decorations. Then she fills the tank, turns on the filter, and begins putting in the fish.

The fish tank looks so beautiful! The child is so fascinated with it. Day after day, he looks at the fish as they swim in between and around the rocks, plants, caves, and other decorations.

After a week, the boy notices something. There is a fish that always hangs around a corner next to a plant ornament and does not swim freely around the tank. He tells his mother what he has observed.

'Oh, I used to put it in a very small glass bowl with that plant ornament. It probably didn't realize it's in a bigger tank with new things now.'

What is the bowl that you've kept yourself in?

Break your metaphorical bowl. If you wish to step outside your boundaries while still being tied to your limiting beliefs, you will be worn down by your inner friction and never go as fast or as far. To start and get out, you must identify your limiting beliefs.

The first step to letting go and overcoming your limiting beliefs is to be aware that they exist. I spoke about one's inner saboteur in Chapter B. If you still need to learn to recognize when your saboteur appears and talks you out of trying, write down the things you believe that you are bad at, that you can't do, or why you choose not to do so. Those are the things that likely shape the base of your limiting beliefs.

There are various ways to overcome limiting beliefs and I'd like to share what I find effective. You can find related information from multiple sources online such as mentoring platforms and coaching blogs.

(i) Recognize that it's just a belief

Not all beliefs are true; otherwise, they would all be called facts. Think about how you came to form this belief.

(ii) Challenge it

Ask yourself—what if my belief is wrong? What am I basing it on? Are there facts to support it? Why do I hold on to it? Push yourself to explore the external realms of your belief or, even better, delve into the opposite of your belief and look from that perspective. Envision the possibilities that open up once you get out of your box and broaden your mind.

(iii) Recognize how your limiting beliefs are negatively impacting your life

Are you going to stay stuck, alone, poor, or unhappy? If your beliefs don't work for you, change them, and see what happens.

(iv) Adopt new beliefs

Get creative. Nothing is stopping you except your own mind. It's not easy to transition from one belief to another, especially if the former has stayed with you till now. But, if you don't try, you have nothing. Start by listing alternative beliefs that are appropriate for you, that can help you improve your situation, that stretch you, that you see work for people you know, or that you are curious about. When you start to plant seeds and think about something, you slowly and subconsciously change your thought process, attention, actions, and decisions to mirror the new beliefs that you are trying to adopt.

(v) Put your beliefs to the test

Like with new recipes or purchases, you test out your new beliefs. For example, if your new belief is: 'I have the time to get fit', set aside thirty minutes daily for a walk and establish a habit from there. If it doesn't work out, try another belief from the ones you listed. It's like trial and error; you fail and you figure it out. If your new belief works out well, condition yourself to this belief and see how far it takes you. Nothing is static forever. Always question and expand the realm of your beliefs. Have the courage to explore and grow.

(vi) Cement your new growth mindset

Be proud of your personal development. Breaking out of the glass bowl is difficult, but you did it.

The shift worker and his colleague

Terence does shift work at a customer support centre and struggles with work-life balance. He comes to work in a grumpy mood and leaves work in a grumpy mood.

Terence observes that his colleague Alan is in an upbeat mood almost all the time. He finds it incredible and decides to speak to Alan during lunch.

'Alan, I can't help but notice that you seem cheerful every day. How do you do it? I hate working shifts. I hate morning shifts because I have to wake up early to come to work, and I hate evening shifts because I can't go for dinner with my friends and family.'

Smiling, Alan responds, 'Well, I enjoy morning shifts because I have the evenings to spend time with friends and family. I enjoy evening shifts because I have the whole day to do my errands and other activities without the crowd.'

After hearing from Alan, Terence was a brand-new man.

Choose a perspective that best serves you and brings balance and contentment. How you look at things makes a difference. Like how music changes the mood in the room, your perspective does the same. Exploring different perspectives enables you to look at the same situation from different angles, thus forming new feelings, thoughts, insights, and experiences. The situation will remain the same but how you look at it or react to it will have an enormous impact on your experience, emotions, and even the outcome.

Release your brakes. Replace your limiting beliefs. Change your negative perspectives. Go for it. Go for the goal you intend to reach.

To quote Mark Twain, 'Twenty years from now, you will be more disappointed by the things you didn't do than by the ones you did.'

Nothing is more dreadful than waking up one day in cold realization, thinking, 'I wished I had.'

This brings us back to that moment on Maria Island.

Standing still and gazing at the top, I realized how much I wanted to be there. And so, without hesitation, I stopped descending, turned around, and started climbing.

Moral of the story:

Don't let anything stop you from unleashing your potential and reaching your goals.

There is a *world of difference* between feeling satisfied and feeling on top of the world.

Trust me. I have been on top of the world that day.

Key takeaways

- Self-limiting beliefs reside in our conscious and subconscious, stopping us from advancing towards our goals.
- These beliefs manifest as compensatory narratives to defend the status quo, such as 'I can be satisfied with less', 'This is not worth it', or 'I don't deserve this'.
- Breaking free of limiting beliefs requires a mindset shift. Challenge the current beliefs that hold you back; they are often the critical voices in your head that tell you not to dream or do it.
- Success is possible with positive thinking and a growth mindset.

Chapter V
Values Come First

'The true perfection of man lies not in what man has, but in what man is.'

—Oscar Wilde, author, poet, and
playwright known for his wit and flamboyance

I get stumped when people question what my values are. This scenario happens mostly during interviews. They are not tricky or difficult questions, but straightforward ones such as 'What are your values?'

I guess I just never thought this through!

Anyway, after a few hiccups, I decided to research the topic of values and hope to identify mine. It's not as simple as searching online for the list of common values and picking the ones that make you sound cool. Values lie deep in our psyche and often stem from our upbringing, culture, education, and experiences. They represent what's important to us and what we care about.

If you value freedom, you will prefer working for a company that allows flexibility. If you value honesty, you may react severely to someone who lied. Values show up more often than you think, and they have a profound impact on your day-to-day life and relationships with people.

Unearth your values

To identify your values, you require a deeper contemplation on why you take certain actions, choose certain decisions, or how you react to certain matters, people, and circumstances. During my professional coach certification with the Co-Active Training Institute, I've learnt different ways to mine and identify key values of others and my own. It was quite a revelation! I highly recommend this approach.

- **Experiences:** Think through why a certain experience is meaningful to you. What is it about the experience you value?
- **Life purpose:** When you talk about your life purpose, you inadvertently reveal what matters most to you and the underlying values that come with it.
- **Emotions:** What makes you angry or upset? What values of yours are being stepped on? Similarly, what makes you happy or appreciative? What values are being honoured?
- **Role model:** Who do you admire? Is the person living your values?
- **Vision:** When you envision a compelling future, you also hold a vision encompassing values and elements important to you.

The above categories are just the tip of the iceberg. There are many ways to uncover the values of yourself and others. Pay attention to common daily occurrences such as conversations, preferences, and habits. Over time, you'll observe patterns and be surprised by how much you can uncover.

Why your goals must be congruent with your values

Another priceless insight I learned during my certification was that values are like the inner GPS that guides you onto a fulfilling path. Values are intangible. You can't see them. But when you do something that honours your values, you feel right and balanced.

Conversely, have you ever emerged victorious in a situation but felt no real joy? Once the high point wavers, emptiness sets in. When your actions and goals are against and not congruent with your values, you feel the tension resulting from your inner conflict.

Undoubtedly, upholding our values all the time can be tiring, especially if we are obsessed with pursuing an outcome. Of course, we can all brush aside our values from time to time to gain an advantage or finish a mission. We probably don't think that there is a problem bearing some dissonance. However, the longer we run the tab of dissonance, the higher the price we pay. In the end, the bill is a life of discontentment and void.

Choosing to live a life based on personal values is not easy. While honouring our values brings us fulfilment, it's not always the path taken.

We grew up in a world shaped by our family, by the media, by our environment, and basically in a society that celebrates in dramatic fashion billionaires, celebrities, and even new iPhones! We have been conditioned since youth to chase after what this kind of society advocates. We often make choices based on what is most practical, what pleases our loved ones, and what makes us happy. While fundamentally, we all want to be happy, there is a *difference between being happy and being fulfilled.*

Happiness is a by-product of a fulfilling life

Happiness isn't a synonym for fulfilment. Many things can make us happy—eating ice cream on a hot day, completing a difficult task, winning a competition—the list goes on. But the feeling of happiness is short-lived. I don't feel happy about a project I delivered three months ago. Once done, it's done.

Fulfilment is different. It goes deeper and longer. I don't necessarily feel happy about writing every day, but I feel highly fulfilled by the work. For every book I sell, I will be happy. For every life I've impacted positively, I will feel fulfilled, and I will keep on generating new content. I hope the messages in my book can inspire and spur people to achieve their goals, and in turn, these people will pay it forward to other people and so on. Fulfilment comes from doing something that has meaning and is purposeful to us.

When we are buried under external expectations and standards, we lose sight of what's truly important to us. By finding out our values and connecting with them, we are clearer about the choices we need to make to live a more fulfilling life.

Values work behind the scenes, unbeknown to you

I'm glad I researched what values are about, although I only did a serious excavation of my own values much later. Upon reflecting on them, I realized two things: firstly, my value of optimism helped me maintain a positive attitude during difficult times and influenced how I acted and reacted. Secondly, when I acted and made decisions aligned with my values, it brought me a sense of peace and order.

During the COVID-19 pandemic in my country, every 'non-essential business' was shut down. For a lengthy period, there wasn't much to do regarding entertainment. Socializing was highly restricted and at times, prohibited. As an extrovert, I thought the pandemic would affect me adversely. There were some frustrations, but during most of the shutdown period, I was really fine. I saw it as an opportunity to challenge myself to experience something different and be more connected internally. With wellness being another personal value, I replaced entertainment with sports. I replaced dining at restaurants with cooking nutritious food at home. I did more yoga and meditation. I actually lost 5 kg during the pandemic and became fitter physically and mentally by being active and eating healthy!

The test came when I lost my job due to restructuring brought about by the pandemic. I admit that I was devastated by my job loss. However, as soon as the initial shock was over, I thought about how to make the best use of this situation. In the end, by staying optimistic, I made massive progress in my personal development. With more time to myself, I furthered my French, embarked on my coaching journey, and started this book while at the same time looking for new jobs. I would not have pushed myself to do what I wanted and accomplished this much when I had a full-time job and other external distractions such as frequent travelling and socializing.

Everything starts to make sense when your values get clearer.

Follow your North Star

As mentioned, values impact your choices and behaviour. There's a reason why job interviewers like to ask questions to look for values. If boldness is one of your values, you will likely be less risk-averse when making decisions or taking action. On the other hand, if you value security, you are more cautious in your approach and may look for alternatives. There's no right or wrong. It's just a matter of values.

Knowing your values put you on a big step towards your North Star—a life of fulfilment and purpose. You now have your GPS to guide you to the desired path; what's needed is for you to set the right goals and take the right actions to live fully to your life purpose. Choosing to prioritize your values over temptations sometimes requires sacrifice and a willingness to bear the criticism, the uncertainty, or the initial discomfort to take an alternate path. You will face naysayers, but all those will pass if you are clear and firm on your values. Eventually, harmony and fulfilment will take over.

'Personal leadership is the process of keeping your vision and values before you and aligning your life to be congruent with them.'

—Stephen Covey, educator, businessperson, keynote speaker, and author of *The 7 Habits of Highly Effective People*

The value of your values will justify itself. Stay true.

Key takeaways

- Knowing our values is crucial because they represent what's important to us.
- Identifying our values requires us to reflect on why we take certain actions, make certain decisions, and how we react to matters, people, and circumstances.
- Our actions and goals should be congruent with our values. Misalignment leads to inner conflict and discontentment. Understanding and connecting our values with our choices enable us to live more fulfilling lives.

Chapter W

Who is the person in the mirror?

'Mirror, mirror on the wall, I'll always get up after I fall. Whether I run, walk, or have to crawl, I'll set my goals and achieve them all.'

—Chris Butler, Co-Founder & COO
of Power of Positivity®

If you pay attention around you, the rule of three is omnipresent—small, medium, big; the *Three Little Pigs*; the *Three Wise Men*; the *Good, the Bad, and the Ugly*. For this chapter, we have,

the past, the present, and the future.

Before you fully embrace the present, you need to conclude your past. As much as you don't want to be heading into a new year with uncashed cheques or unpaid bills, you don't want to let matters of the past linger and interfere with your present. By understanding yourself on a deeper level and asking powerful, albeit difficult questions, you can evoke clarity, create possibility, reveal new learnings, and generate actions.

So, let's face it.

Take a step back.

The past

Think about your past. It doesn't matter at what exact point in the past. It can be in the past week or decade. You will know how far you want to go back, and you can progress slowly. As you reflect, think about where you were, what you were saying or doing, and how you behaved.

To start, I have some questions that can guide your reflection.

- What were the key junctures during this period?
- What were some of my biggest struggles and achievements?
- What have I done, and what have I not done? What would I have changed?
- What were my proudest and most disappointing moments?
- What did I learn or appreciate most about my experiences, good and bad?

Take as much time as you need in this state. When you reach a natural stopping point, return to the present.

The present

Firstly, congratulate yourself on taking this journey inwards. Reflections generate a wide range of sensations. It's not an easy endeavour to relive your past, especially if some moments were unpleasant, but you were strong enough to face it. Write down your immediate thoughts and emotions that were salient during the process. You can refer to them later if you wish to take appropriate action.

During this time, if you have achieved a degree of self-awareness, that is already quite a feat.

If you have experienced an epiphany, that is even more amazing!

Some of the following may have shown up while you were reflecting.

- An urge to do something.
- A desire to change.
- New awareness and insights.

- Clarity about your emotions and thoughts.
- Heaviness and frustrations.
- Inner peace.
- Joy.

Remain in the present. It's the most powerful dimension and the only dimension where your actions can leave an impact by taking steps to clear the past and shape the future.

To embrace the present and absorb its essence, you must complete the past, including everything that leads up to this present moment. You need to make space for it and wrap up things that should not have stayed with you till now. Otherwise, things get messier, and burdens get heavier when you drag them from one phase to another.

The rule of three manifests again

Concluding your past can be handled at three levels. The first level involves finishing lingering chores. These chores are the type that can be completed easily with more time, less procrastination, or hired help. They tend to accumulate because of your lack of attention to them, bad habits, or just plain unwillingness.

Nothing is more annoying than the shadow of an incomplete chore . . .

Believe it or not, your brain keeps track of unfinished chores. They are like bills that you can't ignore paying. Eventually, they accumulate and may cause serious disruptions. Completion of these chores allows the lightness and nimbleness to move forward. Examples of such chores are:

- Finishing filing your taxes and sorting other documents.

- Figuring out what to do with old items.
- Winding up an online course.
- Spring cleaning your house.
- Fixing your broken oven.

The approaches to handling such chores are straightforward. I first got acquainted with this 4D time management concept in Jack Canfield's book *How to Get from Where You Are to Where You Want to Be*. Some sources credited Daniel Johnson as the creator of this concept in his 1991 book *Career Comeback: Taking Charge of Your Career*. The 4D method is used widely to overcome procrastination.

- Drop it (for tasks that are distractions and aren't worth your time and money. Examples are unnecessary meetings and requests).
- Delay it (for non-urgent tasks that do not need to be handled immediately).
- Delegate it (for tasks that can be undertaken by someone with more expertise or can deliver the same outcome. Examples are apartment cleaning or other routine matters).
- Do it (for tasks that you must do after dropping, delaying, and delegating the rest).

Don't wait on it. Deal with it.

. . . or more taxing than the weight of unresolved decisions

The second level points to matters that are more complex. You are stuck or letting a critical decision hang because you are not sure how to deal with it, you fear the consequences once you deal with it, or you face personal mental blocks. Examples of these matters include:

- Redressing a wrong.
- Firing a person.
- Ending a relationship.
- Switching jobs.
- Moving to another city or country.

Ironically, choosing to wait is a decision. However, the mixed emotions that come with choosing to wait don't diminish; they multiply every day until you decide and act. Because these matters are more complex than annoying chores, there are no straightforward, bulletproof approaches. Luckily, I have some suggestions that can help you work through them.

(i) Be clear about what you are trying to achieve

List your objectives. The clearer you are about the outcome, the less you avoid making the decision. The truth is, you can never be 100 per cent certain. A way to support your confidence behind that decision is to go ahead and decide, wait a few days, and then revisit that decision. If there is no factual reason to go against your original decision, act on it. The bottom line is, until you act on it, all you have are doubt and assumptions. Don't be eaten up by what's not real.

(ii) Consider options as well as the pros and cons of each decision

Push yourself to face it. You may not reach a final decision, but considering each part thoroughly makes you more aware of competing viewpoints and can process the conundrum more effectively.

(iii) Distance yourself from your decisions

It's hard to think straight when you are too close to the matter. You can do so spatially or temporally. For the former, view yourself from a third party's perspective. Imagine you are advising a friend in the same situation. For the latter, imagine yourself in one, ten, or twenty years from a more fulfilled state; how would you have advised the current you?

> Clarify your thoughts and assumptions, consider the pros and cons of options, and get some distance.

Regrets don't decompose when you bury them

The third level revolves around something deeper, heavier, and harder to move on. During the reflection, many of you would have come across your regrets, which is sometimes inevitable. No matter what your regrets are, learning from those experiences is an instrumental part of shaping your future self and a key component in goal setting. Concluding your past not only requires you to reflect, but also to accept, forgive, and let go of what had happened. Since the past can never be changed, you must find ways to clear remnants of negative emotions and find peace within yourself to move on.

(i) Seek closure

Set an ending point. Once you have grieved the loss, perform a ritual. It can be a 'fire ceremony' to burn a symbolic object or write what you wish to let go of on a balloon and set it free. Devise an act to seal off the undesirable past and say goodbye forever.

(ii) Make amends

You have hurt people, and you wish to atone for your deeds. Decide how you want to do so, be it a genuine apology or an offer to fix a mistake. You may or may not repair the relationship, but it can be a powerful healing step knowing that you have attempted to right the wrong.

(iii) Change for the better and commit to it

Determine the areas of improvement and act. Nothing is more evident than concrete actions to ensure you don't make the same mistakes. Just remember, don't hang on for too long. Complete the actions, the decisions, and the past. Give your present the attention it deserves.

The way to make the past right is to live the present well.

The future

From now on, move forward with purpose. It's time to envision your future.

- What are your goals?
- Who do you aspire to be?
- How will you feel at that moment?

Proceed with intention.

- What do you need to stop doing?
- What do you need to keep doing?
- What do you need to start doing?

Look in the mirror and ask yourself—what did you do today that makes you proud? Be true. Let there be no excuses.

When your future self assesses you today, I hope you can face the person in the mirror with admiration.

'The happiest man on earth would look into the mirror and see only himself, exactly as he is.'
>   —Professor Albus Dumbledore, a character in
>   J.K. Rowling's *Harry Potter* series, on the
>   Mirror of Erised, a magical mirror
>   that shows the deepest desires of one's heart.

Key takeaways

- Our lives consist of three stages—the past, the present, and the future. We need to conclude each stage before moving on to the next.
- Reflecting on past experiences helps one gain clarity, uncover insights, ignite actions, or surface regrets and pain.
- Concluding the past allows one to embrace the present fully. To do so, one must complete unfinished chores, settle unresolved decisions, sort out complex matters, or make amends.
- Once the previous stage is completed, one can embrace the present and move forward with intention.

Chapter X
Xerox Your Moments

'Take care of all your memories. For you can't relive them.'
—Bob Dylan, singer-songwriter,
and recipient of the Nobel Prize for
Literature in 2016

As a child, I watched a fantasy film called *The NeverEnding Story II*, and I cried and cried. In the film, a boy named Bastian is transported to an imaginary world Fantasia where he must join forces with his friends to stop an evil sorceress from controlling Fantasia and save the empress.

If you are wondering what's so heartbreaking about the movie, the part that had me in tears was seeing the evil sorceress trick the protagonist Bastian into making a wish, resulting in him losing a memory each time he did that. In the end, he was left with two memories—one each of his mother and father. I was so scared that Bastian would lose all his memories and forget all the people and the moments with them that mattered to him. Fortunately, the film had a happy ending, but the potential fear of losing all memories was so acute that I must make a point for their preservation.

Without memories, life is but a two-dimensional snapshot

Why do we take pictures and videos during vacations, occasions, or gatherings? It's because we want to keep those moments as vivid as possible in our memory. But why? What's the driving force behind this?

Memories connect.

Across time and generations, memories connect people, culture, and history. Memories enable us to remember people no longer with us, honour our culture and heritage, be cognizant of shifts and transformations over different periods, and preserve the past for posterity.

It's our memory of things that affect how we assess past events, how we decide and act now, and how we determine the next steps. It's the glue that binds the various pieces of our lives. It's what makes us whole. It's what gives us depth.

When I lost my job in 2018, I was devastated. I felt like a failure, had massive self-doubts, and had no idea where or how to move on from that space.

Then, something unexpected happened. I don't know what brought me there, but I actually went back to the neighbourhood I grew up in. I had this urge to reminisce about the past and connect with one of the happiest times of my life.

I took the same bus from the metro station, and as I stopped at the same spot near my old block, I felt my heart just opened up. So many things have changed, yet so many things have remained. I saw a new green garden below my block where residents planted flowers and vegetables and a newly renovated playground. As I went up to the fourteenth storey where I used to live, I recognized an old neighbour who walked with a limp. He had grey hair and some wrinkles but still looked mostly the same after even twenty years!

Amazing.

I walked along the corridor where I once played Hopscotch, zero point, and hide-and-seek with my childhood buddies. I then walked to the minimart where my buddies and I used to buy Paddle Pop ice creams. The owners are still there! I continued to my favourite hawker centre; the man with a glass eye was still running the fruit stall! Unbelievable! It's like time has stood still in some instances. For the rest of the day, I went to my primary school, high school, and basically all the places where I used to hang out and just soaked in those moments.

The nostalgia was beyond words. Remembering my humble yet joyful beginning was a strong rejuvenating force for me to face the future, albeit how uncertain I felt then. I should not be defined as a person who has lost her job but by what I love, cherish, and hope.

One of the greatest legacies is the memories you can give yourself.

Modest Ming

I bumped into an old classmate when I walked past my high school. I will call him Ming.

When we spoke then, Ming was a finance director at a multinational conglomerate and lived in a neighbourhood far away from our old school. I was curious to know what he was doing in the vicinity and was surprised to hear that he occasionally goes back to his old flat where he stays overnight for a day or two. Ming mentioned that although he currently lives in a bungalow, he never sold the flat he grew up in. He didn't even renovate his flat, but merely repainted the walls and repaired broken fixtures. His old home reminded him of simpler times and his roots. He even brought his children along at times and let them experience the days of his modest upbringing and connect with old neighbours.

'I want them to appreciate what they have now and understand the value of hard work and community through learning about the past', Ming said.

Look back and celebrate, look forward and celebrate

Memories make comfy cushions for old age but they are more than just for nostalgic recall. Memories are a well of vast information, powerful knowledge, and deep emotions.

They hold rich details about what happened, what we did, and how we felt. They also reinvigorate hope and motivation for our future. They contain the key to unleashing our dreams.

By revisiting past experiences, we unearth new insights and ignite unexpected reactions that could be important inputs in the journey towards our goals. Our memory is the thread that links our past and present and will continue to weave its way into our future identity. It fuels our momentum and steers our actions.

Luckily, we don't have to remember events and experiences the old way. We now have the equipment and technology to capture precious moments, duplicate unlimited copies for sharing, and store them digitally and physically forever. If you wish to relive palpably certain moments that are special to you and be able to access those memories via a 'touch', one creative way is to store items related to those moments, be it a movie ticket, a card, or a toy in a big jar or an empty box. Decorate and label the box or jar as you wish. Have that jar or box dedicated to happy, inspirational, romantic, victorious, and many other cherished times. Don't let special moments become mere mental images that pale over time.

Photocopy your moments. Preserve your memories. Document your journey. Photos, videos, journals, and even jars of precious items are valuable artefacts to be kept for sentimental, practical, and celebratory purposes as you go forward in your journey.

To quote American children's author and illustrator Dr Seuss, 'Sometimes you will never know the value of a moment, until it becomes a memory.'

And you will only know the value of memories and what they can bring to your present and future when you revisit moments of them.

Key takeaways

- Memories hold rich information and emotions and are the thread that links our past, present, and future.
- Our memory of things affects how we assess people and events, decide and act, and form our future identity.
- Make use of technology to capture precious moments, store them, and share them so we may relive special moments.

Chapter Y
Yes, I Can!

'Yes, I can!'

—A trainer in a career counselling session
that I attended

The above encouragement concluded that session.

The first time I heard about affirmations was during that session. Frankly, I wasn't convinced. At that time, I was actively searching for a new job and had no luck for months. One advice from the trainer was to practise affirmations, an intentional form of self-talk in which I tell myself encouraging words to motivate myself to reach my full potential and achieve my goals, yada, yada.

Now you know why I was sceptical. However, I figured I had nothing to lose, so I gave it a go. While at it, I decided to put in the effort and do it right to test its efficacy.

Indeed, I noticed a gradual change. I felt less anxious and more at peace with myself. By expressing positive statements, I began to assess things differently. I started to link things associated with my statements, conceiving possibilities, solutions, and alternatives in the process. I became more resilient, confident, and, some say, pleasant! In the end, the job offers came.

Who knew?

The science behind affirmations

It's hard to pinpoint where and when affirmations started as they have roots in ancient religions. Various sources have cited the affirmations, as we know them today, from the work of French psychotherapist Emile Coue. The key point is—don't underestimate the power of affirmations. Affirmations are positive statements that can reframe your thinking and support you in creating the outcome you want. There's a scientific explanation for this—neuroplasticity—the ability of the brain to change and rewire itself in response to intrinsic or extrinsic factors.

A 2016 study titled 'Self-affirmation activates brain systems associated with self-related processing and reward and is reinforced by future orientation', demonstrated that neurocognitive processes can be strengthened with self-affirmation.

Our brain is malleable and can reorganize neural pathways and create new connections and neurons based on our thought patterns. Hence, we want to influence our brain to develop in our desired path.

Affirmations are powerful because they work from within. Most of the time, we are not conscious of our inner voice, our self-talk. Yet, this inner voice stealthily guides our thoughts, emotions, and actions. This inner voice can be both positive and negative, and we certainly wouldn't want it to focus on the negative because what we think on a regular basis has an impact on our thought patterns and brain structure. Our actions follow our convictions. Simply put, the more we tell ourselves we are not good enough, the more we believe it and act in a way that confirms our beliefs.

On the other hand, we can do the opposite! We want to train our brains to concentrate on the positive. By saying our affirmations out loud, we are consciously appreciating and giving credit to ourselves, thereby cultivating a kinder self-view. When we repeatedly think and say something, we build and strengthen a new neural pathway in our brain. Neurons that are frequently used develop stronger connections and adapt to the changing environment, making it easier for us to form positive thought patterns over time.

Create the reality you want

I still remember one of my first few affirmations, 'I am enjoying my work, and I'm respected for my skills and experience.'

Words turned into belief; belief turned into reality. Whether it's science, time, or luck, affirmations did play an unexpected role in my job pursuits, and I'm thankful to have learnt this technique.

To start practicing affirmations, think about areas in your life where you would like to see positive changes and results. For your affirmations to be effective, you need to use precise, positive, and realistic phrases that are meaningful to you.

Here are some guidelines that I have picked up from my career counselling session to help one construct an affirmation.

How to construct affirmations

1. Affirmations are about *you*. Start with 'I' or 'I am'. Saying 'Readers enjoy my book' is not the same as 'I write captivating content that makes readers laugh', or 'I am creating captivating content for my readers'. You are at the centre and need to be the sentence's subject. By saying 'I' or 'I am', you are training your brain to follow your instructions to make your desires happen.

2. Say your affirmations in the present tense. Convince your brain to think that it's already happening. There is a world of difference in the mindset between 'I am in a loving and healthy relationship', versus 'I will be in a loving and healthy relationship'. It may be subtle, but your brain can pick up the difference. Say your affirmation as if you have already achieved it and are relishing the moment.

3. Use positive words. If I say, 'Don't think of a pink elephant', what do you think of? A pink elephant! The same goes for affirmations. State what you want, not what you don't want. Instead of saying, 'I don't fear public speaking', say 'I express myself confidently on stage'.

4. Brevity is key. Be concise with your affirmations so you can remember them easily.
5. Be precise. Like with goal setting, you need to be clear with your affirmations. 'I am walking among lavender fields in Hokkaido during summer' is more vivid than 'I am on vacation in Japan'.
6. I spoke about the power of visualization in the first chapter. Visualization is a key component in affirmations to aid clarity. Start the affirmation process by forming vivid mental images, engaging as many senses as possible while visualizing. Think about:

    •   The situation you are in: What are your surroundings like? What are the things you see? Visualize the colours, the objects, and as many other details as you can.
    •   The sound of the surrounding: If you are visualizing yourself in your beach house facing the ocean, imagine the sounds of the waves or the voices of people chattering.
    •   The sensations: How do you feel when you are there? If you are still visualizing your beach house, imagine the warmth of the sun and the sea breeze on your skin.
    •   The scents: If you want your visualization to be more palpable, you can use essential oils with the right aroma to stimulate the visualization. Just ensure you don't have a medical condition that triggers any adverse effects.

    The clarity of your visualization will help you to craft a precise affirmation.
7. Inject dynamism into your affirmations. Using the vacation example, a way to immerse yourself in your affirmations is to add powerful adjectives or verbs.

Emotions bring things to life and make them easier to remember. A way to enhance the above affirmation is to say, 'I am rejuvenated walking among lavender fields in Hokkaido during summer!'

Pair your affirmations with power poses

Embodying your belief is key. Besides affirmations, I used another technique called 'power posing'. I learned about power posing in the same career counselling session, and upon further exploration, I read that this is a concept popularized by Amy Cuddy in a 2012 TED talk that went viral.

Power posing suggests that our posture influences how we feel and behave. If we place our bodies in positions that we mentally associate with being powerful, we will feel and behave in a way that aligns with power. Again, when I first heard about this, I was sceptical. But since I was shaking before a major interview and was desperate to curb my nervousness, I gave power-posing a go.

As I was reciting my affirmations, I shifted my posture to reflect how I would feel if I were successful. I did the well-known 'Wonder Woman' pose—standing with my feet apart, lifting my chest and head, and my hands on my hips.

Through that pose, I had hoped to embody confidence before I went for interviews. True enough, I noticed the difference in the flow of energy through my body. My heart wasn't racing as fast, and I calmed down almost immediately. I might not have transformed into Wonder Woman, but I definitely felt more ready and emboldened by the mission ahead.

If you think about it, postures do affect how we feel. My schoolteacher used to call out students who were slumping on their desks. She would say, 'Sit up straight! You will feel more energized!' There is a reason behind this. If we slump, how would we want our energy to flow smoothly? More importantly, we are perceived by how we carry ourselves. Powerful postures signal to people that we are confident, dependable, strong, and ready to take charge.

Additional ways to strengthen your affirmations

(i) Make the invisible, visible

Write them down. Record your affirmations. Put your affirmations on your screensaver, fridge, mirror, and everywhere. In Chapter A, I mentioned you need to remind yourself every day and every chance of your goals. The same applies for affirmations. There are countless methods to ensure that you see your affirmations easily to stay focused on that reality you crave.

(ii) Action

Affirmations must be backed with actions. You need to instil new habits, beliefs, and behaviours for affirmations to be effective. When I wished for a highly sought-after job, I didn't just recite my affirmations and wing my chances during interviews. I put in the effort to prepare and practise and combined my preparations with my affirmations to make it through the stressful times. Think of affirmations as a step towards change, not the change itself.

(iii) Be grateful

Your mindset shifts when you look out for the positive things in life. Whether you look for the merit in a situation or reframe the adverse situation more sanguinely, you nurture an optimistic outlook on life. Optimism encourages you to stay motivated and work towards your goals. If you believe in the law of attraction, a pseudoscience based on the belief that similar things attract one another, you want to emphasize your energy and thoughts on the positives to invite more like experiences.

(iv) Try it out, sincerely

Do it right. Do it with belief. Nothing shifts until you believe. By trying, you potentially have everything to gain. At the very least, you will feel calmer as you seek to disrupt negative thoughts and overcome them with positive ones. You are permitting more upbeat energy to flow through, developing a greater appreciation of yourself, and diffusing this vigour across multiple aspects of your life.

Saying that you (I) *can* achieve your goal is the ultimate step to achieving your (my) goal.

Yes, I can!

Key takeaways

- Affirmations are positive statements that can reframe how you think and influence your inner voice, thoughts, and emotions to support you in creating the desired outcome.

- Neuroplasticity is the scientific explanation behind the effectiveness of affirmations, which help rewire the brain and create new connections and neurons based on thought patterns.
- To construct effective affirmations, be concise and precise, use positive words, say them in the present tense, and use visualization to aid clarity.
- Power poses strengthen affirmations and confidence by embodying the energy associated with power.

Chapter Z
Zenith after Zenith

'It always seems impossible until it's done.'
—Nelson Mandela, anti-Apartheid activist
and first Black President of South Africa

Just a little more . . .

Remember what I just said about affirmations?

You are here!

You have achieved what you set out to do.

How do you feel?

Take a moment to let your emotions sink in before reading this final chapter.

Here's an important reminder. As much as this book centres on achieving your goals, the action is not an end in itself.

Every conclusion has a new beginning. There are always more goals to achieve. The ultimate question is, *what are you pursuing*?

'Arriving at one goal is the starting point to another.'
—John Dewey, philosopher, psychologist, and
educational reformer

Why you should always have a goal

I used to be afraid of ageing.

Right now, if a genie were to tell me that he would grant me a wish to go back in time and restart my life at eighteen (without knowing lottery numbers or the share prices of companies, of course!), I wouldn't take that wish. It may seem counter-intuitive, but many people don't want to go back to being eighteen, especially if they were young and foolish then!

I mean, we all want to *look* young, but that is a different topic for a different book. When you have spent your life doing something meaningful, you don't want to go back and be young again. Instead, you want to go forward by doing more, experiencing more, learning more, and achieving more.

I came to realize that ageing is not decay; it's growth, it's learning, and it's also giving back, but only if you allow ageing to reveal its own significance and sophistication.

And so, one way to embrace moving forward without fear of ageing and growing wiser is . . . to set goals!

Setting goals presents us with a roadmap and motivation to move forward. It helps us be focused and organized to better devote our time and resources to the things that matter to us.

Extrinsic and intrinsic motivation

In their work on motivation, psychologists Edward L. Deci and Richard M. Ryan, posit that there are two main types of motivations—intrinsic and extrinsic. With intrinsic and extrinsic motivations come the two types of goals, and they map onto different definitions of satisfaction. The goals you choose to pursue differ according to your needs and wants at that time.

Examples of extrinsic versus intrinsic motivations:

Extrinsic	Intrinsic
Studying to obtain good grades	Studying because you are curious about the subject
Starting a business because you want to make money	Starting a business because you want to solve a need and create value
Volunteering to fulfil a requirement	Volunteering because it brings you joy and fulfilment

Exercising to look good	Exercising to enhance well-being
Hanging out with someone because you want to be seen as 'cool'	Hanging out with someone because you enjoy the company

Extrinsic goals are achievement-oriented and motivated by external influences. This type of goal points to a prize, an outcome, or an outward form of approval and evaluation that makes you feel exuberant and proud when you achieve them, such as getting into a prestigious college, buying your first car, or hitting 10,000 followers on Instagram.

While extrinsic goals can be fantastic achievements, they don't provide lasting fulfilment. Sure, you can argue that you will just set more goals, such as graduating summa cum laude or buying a fancier car, but you risk trapping yourself in an endless cycle of extrinsic pursuits. When you fail to reach them, you become discouraged because your self-esteem depends on how much you achieve and the presumed admiration from others. However, it's worth highlighting that achieving extrinsic goals can lead to eventual fulfilment when you use the outcomes to realize other intrinsic goals. An example will be to use your money to help the sick and frail or to pursue other passions.

Intrinsic goals, on the other hand, are goals that fulfil core human needs. You pursue these goals because they are meaningful, pertain to your passion, interests, core values, personal growth, and connection, and nourish you psychologically. There are no other incentives apart from doing it because you want to and enjoy it. Even if your intrinsic goal does not lead to a prize or a certain outcome, you will still find satisfaction through growth and self-actualization in the process. In this case, achieving the goal is satisfying in itself.

If I'm writing this book because I want to be rich and famous by selling millions of copies, I'm extrinsically motivated.

If I'm writing this book because I love to motivate and inspire and hope my messages can positively impact people's lives, I'm intrinsically motivated.

Can a person be both extrinsically and intrinsically motivated? Of course!

There's always an underlying motive behind a goal. You will know in your heart what type of goal you gravitate towards. In my case, if I derive external success from writing this book, it will not be deliberate but as a by-product of my intrinsic goal—*to inspire people to become a better version of themselves.* By penning down my experience and lessons in goal pursuits, I hope my messages can galvanize people to find and reach their own goals.

The chain reaction of goals

Once you achieve your first goal, be it big or small, you are highly likely to set your sights on the next one. One goal initiates the next. The momentum keeps going. Because of this motion, you will uncover opportunities that you never imagined possible! As this path unfolds gradually, at different times and stages, you'll pursue different things, find different things, rediscover different things, and hopefully continue to achieve different and bigger things.

The most beautiful part about this chain reaction is that you will be transformed! To go after bigger goals, you'll have to develop greater capacity and self-mastery. You will develop new competencies and attitudes. Repeating Ralph Waldo Emerson's quote from Chapter B, 'The mind, once stretched by a new idea, never returns to its original dimensions'. And so will you. When you stretch your goals, you will be stretched by them too, into a bigger and better person! Forever.

Be proud of who you have become in the process.

Do what you love, or learn to love what you do

Welcome the full range of emotions. In pursuing our goals, there will be periods of intensity and serenity, gains and losses, joy and grief. You are not always going to enjoy every moment and every task. But remember why you do it and hold that *why* close to you. The ride itself teaches you more than the destination. Extrinsic or intrinsic, no matter what type of goals you are going after, what matters most is that you have done something that made you grow, learn, be more connected, and bring meaning and value to yourselves and others along the way.

I hope you have enjoyed reading the book, and I wish you all the best as you march towards zenith after zenith in your journey.

'You can motivate by fear, and you can motivate by reward. But both those methods are only temporary. The only lasting thing is self-motivation.'
—Homer Rice, former American football player
and coach

Go for it! Most importantly, enjoy the ride.

'Well that was an emotional rollercoaster.'

CartoonStock.com

Key takeaways

- Achieving your goals is not an end in itself. It's important to set new goals to move forward in a focused manner.
- Going after bigger and better goals develops your capacity, self-mastery, competencies, and attitude, transforming you into a bigger and better person.
- There are two types of goals—extrinsic and intrinsic. Extrinsic goals are achievement-oriented and motivated by external influences and rewards, while intrinsic goals fulfil core human needs and satisfy you psychologically.
- No matter what you are going after, enjoy the ride. The most important thing is learning, growing, finding meaning, and bringing value to yourself and others along the journey.

Supplement your reading with coaching

One way to supplement reading this book is to pair it with coaching to apply the lessons more effectively. Coaching is a creative and stimulating process that aims to help you improve your performance, focusing on bringing you from your current state to an ideal state by evoking transformation at various stages.

As a certified coach, I employ several techniques and tools to enable my clients to clarify their goals, identify their blockers, values, strengths, and even unspoken fears, and guide them to access their inner and external resources. Hence they become more aware of what they can or need to do to facilitate their journey towards personal and professional goals. Coupled with nearly two decades of experience in programme management work for top multinational companies, I am well-versed in various strategies and tactics to achieve major goals within tight timelines to aid or mentor you in your journey.

If you wish to deepen your learning and establish a tailored and stronger pathway to achieve your goals, please reach out. I will gladly partner with you in your journey towards an ideal and fulfilling life.

Suggested Reading and Resources

Reading has been an integral part of my personal growth. I would like to list the resources that provided me the inspiration and information for my book.

Kimsey-House Henry, Kimsey-House Karen, Sandahl Phil, Whitworth Laura. *Co-Active Coaching: The Proven Framework for Transformative Conversations at Work and in Life.* 4th edition. John Murray Press, 2018.

Senge, Peter M. *The Fifth Discipline: The Art and Practice of the Learning Organization.* Random House Books, 2006.

Greene, Robert. *The 48 Laws of Power.* New York: Penguin Books, 2000.

Covey, Stephen R. *The 7 Habits of Highly Effective People: Power Lessons in Personal Change.* 15th edition. Free Press, 2004.

Canfield Jack. *How to Get from Where You Are to Where You Want to Be: The 25 Principles of Success.* New York: Harper Element, 2005.

Eker, T. Harv. *Secrets of the Millionaire Mind: Think rich to get rich.* London: Piatkus, 2005.

Welch, Jack and Suzy Welch. *Winning.* New York: HarperBusiness Publishers, 2005.

'Everything You Need to Know About SMART Goals'. *Achieve It.* https://www.achieveit.com/resources/blog/everything-you-need-to-know-about-smart-goals/.

Doran, G.T. 'There's a SMART Way to Write Management's Goals and Objectives'. *Journal of Management Review*, 1981, 70, 35–36.

University of Colorado at Boulder. 'Your brain on imagination: It's a lot like reality, study shows.'10 Dec. 2018. *ScienceDaily*. www.sciencedaily.com/releases/2018/12/181210144943.htm

Minds Tool Content Team. 'Visualization: Imagining – and Achieving – Your Goals'. https://www.mindtools.com/a5ycdws/visualization.

Clark, L. Verdelle. 'Effect of Mental Practice on the Development of a Certain Motor Skill.' *The Research Quarterly*, American Association for Health, Physical Education, and Recreation, vol. 31, no. 4, Taylor and Francis, Dec. 1960, pp. 560–69. https://doi.org/10.1080/10671188.1960.10613109.

Kearns, Dwight W., and Jane Crossman. 'Effects of a Cognitive Intervention Package on the Free-Throw Performance of Varsity Basketball Players During Practice and Competition.' *Perceptual and Motor Skills*, vol. 75, no. 3_suppl, SAGE Publishing, Dec. 1992, pp. 1243–53. https://doi.org/10.2466/pms.1992.75.3f.1243.

Queen Mary University of London. 'Mathematicians work out how to predict success in show business.' 4 Jun. 2019. https://www.qmul.ac.uk/media/news/2019/se/mathematicians-work-out-how-to-predict-success-in-show-business.html

Williams, Oliver E., et al. 'Quantifying and Predicting Success in Show Business.' *Nature Communications*, vol. 10, no. 1, Nature Portfolio, Jun. 2019, https://doi.org/10.1038/s41467-019-10213-0.

Cao, Sissi. 'Here's Why Becoming a Lucrative YouTube Star Keeps Getting Harder.' *Observer.com*. 28 Feb. 2018. https://observer.com/2018/02/study-youtube-stars-earnings-us-median-income/.

'Men's Basketball: Probability of Competing beyond High School.' *NCAA.org*, 20 Apr. 2020, https://www.ncaa.org/sports/2015/3/6/men-s-basketball-probability-of-competing-beyond-high-school.aspx.

Milkman, Katherine L., et al. 'Holding the Hunger Games Hostage at the Gym: An Evaluation of Temptation Bundling.' *Management Science*, vol. 60, no. 2, Institute for Operations

Research and the Management Sciences, Feb. 2014, pp. 283–99. https://doi.org/10.1287/mnsc.2013.1784.

Walsh, Karla. 'Habit Stacking—and Why It Might Finally Help Your Behavior Changes Stick'. Reviewed by Gillihan, Seth. PhD. *Everyday Health*. 13 Feb. 2023. https://www.everydayhealth.com/emotional-health/habit-stacking-and-why-it-might-help-your-behavior-changes-stick/.

Scott, S.J. *Habit Stacking: 127 Small Changes to Improve Your Health, Wealth, and Happiness*. Oldtown Publishing LLC. 2017.

Kaizen Institute. 'What is Kaizen™ | Meaning of Kaizen'.

'The Space Between Self-Esteem and Self Compassion: Kristin Neff at TEDxCentennialParkWomen.' Youtube: https://www.youtube.com/watch?v=IvtZBUSplr4. Uploaded by TEDx Talks, 7 Feb. 2013.

Rakshit, Devrupa. "The 'Spotlight Effect' Is When We Think People Are Thinking About Us More Than They Are". *Swaddle*. 31 Aug. 2020.

https://theswaddle.com/the-spotlight-effect-is-when-you-think-people-are-noticing-your-flaws-more-than-they-really-are/.

Miller Earl K., Histed Mark H., Pasupathy Anitha. 'Learning Substrates in the Primate Prefrontal Cortex and Striatum: Sustained Activity Related to Successful Actions.' *Neuron*, vol. 63, no. 2, Cell Press, Jul. 2009, pp. 244–53. https://doi.org/10.1016/j.neuron.2009.06.019.

Yakov Bart, Pierre Chandon, Steven Sweldens, Raquel Seabra de Sousa. 'Renova Toilet Paper: Avant-garde Marketing in a Commoditized Category.' INSEAD Case Study 5685, 28 Jun. 2010

Shields, Arnold. 'Should You Give Up On Cold Calling as a Small Business Marketing Tool?' 10 Sep. 2009. https://www.dolmanbateman.com.au/blog/should-you-give-up-on-cold-calling-as-a-small-business-marketing-tool.

Van Rensburg, Ilse. 'The Top Cold Calling Success Rates for 2023 Explained.' 14 Sep. 2022. https://www.cognism.com/blog/cold-calling-success-rates#:~:text=The%20average%20cold%20calling%20success%20rate%20is%202%25.&text=Depending%20

on%20the%20cold%20calling,an%20isolated%20sales%20call%20 statistic.

Ferris, Tim. 'The Tim Ferris show: LeBron James and His Top-Secret Trainer, Mike Mancias (#349).' Podcast, 27 Nov. 2018. https://tim.blog/2018/11/27/lebron-james-mike-mancias/.

Connley, Courtney. 'LeBron James reveals the nighttime routine that helps him perform 'at the highest level.' 23 Dec. 2018. https://www.cnbc.com/2018/12/21/lebron-james-reveals-the-nighttime-routine-that-sets-him-up-for-success.html.

In, Nan-hie. 'How sleep helps athletes like LeBron James and Roger Federer – and the ways we can get a good night's rest too.' 23 Jul. 2018. https://www.scmp.com/lifestyle/health-wellness/article/2156133/how-sleep-helps-athletes-lebron-james-and-roger-federer.

Clifford, Catherine. 'Olympic hero Michael Phelps says this is the secret to his success.' CNBC, 14 Feb. 2017. https://www.cnbc.com/2017/02/14/olympic-hero-michael-phelps-says-this-is-the-secret-to-his-success.html.

'Why athletes should make sleep a priority in their daily training'. *Fatigue Science.* 4 Sep. 2013. https://fatiguescience.com/blog/infographic-why-athletes-should-make-sleep-a-priority-in-their-daily-training/

'Transforming Dreams Into Successful Business' at the Hong Kong Convention & Exhibition Center for the Young Hong Kong Entrepreneurs. Youtube: https://www.youtube.com/watch?v=JXCPVhJMC0c
Uploaded by Alibaba CEO Daniel, 2 Feb. 2015.

Baumann, Abby. 'Everything You Need to Know About Machine Utilization.' 6 Mar. 2023. https://blog.amper.xyz/everything-you-need-to-know-about-machine-utilization#:~:text=An%20Amper%20customer%20survey%20revealed,depends%20on%20your%20particular%20business.

Lauzier, Jacob. 'Machine Utilization: Track and Improve Equipment Performance.' 18 Aug. 2022. https://www.machinemetrics.com/

blog/machine-utilization#:~:text=While%20all%20these%20 areas%20have,rate%20of%20just%2028%25!.

Ebbinghaus, Hermann. *Memory: A Contribution to Experimental Psychology*, translated by H.A. Ruger and C.E. Bussenius. Teachers College, Columbia University, New York City, 1913.

Mind Tools Content Team. 'Ebbinghaus's Forgetting Curve. Why We Keep Forgetting and What We Can Do About It.' https:// www.mindtools.com/a9wjrjw/ebbinghauss-forgetting-curve.

'Learning "Myth" #1: Ebbinghaus Forgetting Curve'. https:// intelalearning.wordpress.com/2018/07/19/learning-myth-1-ebbinghaus-forgetting-curve/.

'Diminishing returns - Wikipedia'. https://en.wikipedia.org/wiki/ Diminishing_returns

Weiler, Nicholas. 'Your gut – the second brain?' From our neurons to yours. Wu Tsai Neurosciences Institute at Stanford University. Podcast, 16 Feb. 2023. https://neuroscience.stanford.edu/news/ your-gut-second-brain.

Wilding, Melody. 'How to Stop Overthinking and Start Trusting Your Gut.' *Harvard Business Review*. 10 Mar. 2022. https:// hbr.org/2022/03/how-to-stop-overthinking-and-start-trusting-your-gut.

Robson, David. 'Intuition: When is it right to trust your gut instincts?' 4 Apr. 2022. *BBC Worklife*. https://www.bbc.com/ worklife/article/20220401-intuition-when-is-it-right-to-trust-your-gut-instincts.

'6 Steps to Breaking Your Limiting Beliefs'. PushFar. https://www. pushfar.com/article/6-steps-to-breaking-your-limiting-beliefs/.

'How to Overcome Self-Limiting Beliefs.' Integrity. https://www. integritycoaching.co.uk/blog/overcoming-the-challenges-of-headship/self-limiting-beliefs/#:~:text=Self%2Dlimiting%20 beliefs%20are%20the,in%20response%20to%20painful%20 experiences.

Cascio, Christopher N., O'Donnell, Matthew B., Tinney, Francis J., Taylor, Shelley E., Lieberman, Matthew D. 'Self-affirmation

Activates Brain Systems Associated with Self-related Processing and Reward and Is Reinforced by Future Orientation.' *Social Cognitive and Affective Neuroscience*, vol. 11, no. 4, University of Oxford, Apr. 2016, pp. 621–29. https://doi.org/10.1093/scan/nsv136.

London, Sarah. 'The 4Ds of Time Management | Master Your To-Do List'. Hive. 9 May 2022. https://hive.com/blog/4-ds-of-time-management/.

Akter, Shamima. 'Mastering the 4Ds of Time Management'. Time Hackz. 25 May 2021. https://timehackz.com/4-ds-of-time-management/.

Hanscom, David. MD. Reviewed by Lyons, Daniel. M.A. 'Affirmations and Neuroplasticity. Affirmations can help us develop a more optimistic way of looking at ourselves.' 30 Jan. 2020. https://www.psychologytoday.com/sg/blog/anxiety-another-name-pain/202001/affirmations-and-neuroplasticity.

Alleyne, Matthew E. 'The History of Affirmations'. Selfgrowth. https://www.selfgrowth.com/articles/the-history-of-affirmations?no_redirect=true.

Mind Tools Content Team. 'Using Affirmations - Harnessing Positive Thinking'. Mindtools. https://www.mindtools.com/air49f4/using-affirmations.

Smith, S Renee, Harte, Vivian. 'How to Write Your Own Affirmations'. Dummies. 28 Jun. 2021. https://www.dummies.com/article/body-mind-spirit/emotional-health-psychology/emotional-health/general-emotional-health/how-to-write-your-own-affirmations-145446/.

Stevemagness. 'Why Power Posing Works? Exploring Social Psychology.' Science of Running. 31 Jan. 2020. https://www.scienceofrunning.com/2020/01/why-power-posing-works-exploring-social-psychology.html?v=47e5dceea252.

Cuddy, Amy. 'Your body language may shape who you are' [Video]. YouTube. Uploaded by TED. 1 Oct. 2012. https://www.youtube.com/watch?v=Ks-_Mh1QhMc&t=9s.

Schutz, Astrid Y, Bushman, Brad. 'The idea that power poses boost your confidence fell from favor – but a new review of the research calls for a second look.' 12 May. 2022. https://theconversation.com/the-idea-that-power-poses-boost-your-confidence-fell-from-favor-but-a-new-review-of-the-research-calls-for-a-second-look-180541.

Ackerman, Courtney E. Scientifically reviewed by Maike Neuhaus. 'Self Determination Theory and How It Explains Motivation'. Positivepsychology. 21 Jun. 2018. https://positivepsychology.com/self-determination-theory/.

Deci, Edward L., Ryan, Richard M. 'Self-Determination Theory and the Facilitation of Intrinsic Motivation, Social Development, and Well-Being' *American Psychologiust.* University of Rochester. Jan. 2000. 55:1, 68–78. https://selfdeterminationtheory.org/SDT/documents/2000_RyanDeci_SDT.pdf.

O'Hara, Delia. 'The intrinsic motivation of Richard Ryan and Edward Deci'. *American Psychological Association.* 18 Dec. 2017. https://www.apa.org/members/content/intrinsic-motivation.

Acknowledgement

It always takes a team. Writing this book has been a major project of mine for the past two years, but getting the book refined, edited, published and finally out into the hands of readers takes a team.

I wish to first thank my husband, Benjamin, for giving me the space to work on my book and supporting me through this process. I also want to thank my parents and family for their unconditional love and patience. Next, I'd also like to say a big thank you to my friends and the people in my life who have inspired and influenced me in various manners across various stages. You brought important knowledge, stimulating discussions, and whimsical moments that gave breadth and depth to my life. Your experiences and ideas were critical in shaping the content, and I hope your stories will go on to inspire many others.

Lastly, I wish to call out the stellar squad at Penguin Random House SEA. Your vision, dedication, and guidance transformed a manuscript into a meaningful product. Thank you, Nora, for granting me the opportunity to work with you and your team.

I had one of the greatest and most intense moments of my life writing this book and seeing it through to fruition. It was hard work, but nevertheless, pure joy. Thank you all.